THE GREGORIAN EPOCH

Reformation, Revolution, Reaction?

PROBLEMS IN EUROPEAN CIVILIZATION

THE GREGORIAN EPOCH

Reformation, Revolution, Reaction?

217684 F
H

EDITED WITH AN INTRODUCTION BY

Schafer Williams, UNIVERSITY OF MASSACHUSETTS

D. C. HEATH AND COMPANY
Lexington, Massachusetts

Table of Contents

Introduction

THE period lying between the Synod of Sutri (1046) and the Concordat of Worms (1122) is called for convenience "The Age of the Gregorian Reform," or "The Struggle of the Investitures," or "The Conflict between Church and State." Specialists in German national history, German constitutional history, church history, the history of canon law, mediaeval political theory, and mediaeval cultural history have published a huge number of carefully edited contemporary documents as well as countless monographs on the personalities, groups, regions, institutions, currents, questions, and problems lying within or across these seventy-six years.

In these seven and a half decades occurred events of such a momentous nature, at so many levels, and in so many areas of human endeavour that one is justified in stating boldly and categorically: Here are first discernible the most characteristic elements of the European civilization still viable today!

From a geographical point of view the people of Europe were already beginning to generate the waves of exploration and expansion which have remained a continuing pattern of Europe's development to modern times. America had been discovered by daring Viking sea rovers and a flourishing settlement in Greenland was well established; the Salian rulers of Germany were establishing Christian strongholds on the Baltic and pressing the Slavs of the northeast. The dynamic and administratively talented Normans expanded to England and not only obliterated the Byzantine and Saracenic outposts in Italy but also harassed the Eastern Empire in the Balkans and Turkey. Armed, consecrated groups were already driving back the Infidel in the Iberian peninsula and the century would close with the Latin Christian host in the Holy City of Jerusalem. The mere fact that Latin Europe could raise, arm, mount, and send forth the multitude of the First Crusade in 1096 is impressive evidence of the striking increase in that area's population and wealth. It demonstrates dramatically the high "energy level" of eleventh-century European society.

In the realm of the mind, the philosophical and theological inquiries of St. Anselm, Berengarius, and Lanfranc, the momentous re-discovery of Justinian's Roman law belong to this period. The beginning of systematic teaching of Roman law by Irnerius and (at the end of our period) of canon law by Gratian at Bologna, and the rise of the *studium generale* or university, likewise emerge in this brief span. The development of administrative techniques and competence is evidenced by the fact that registers of papal letters, imperial and royal decrees, episcopal registers and account books, and enumerations of people and property like the greatest single mediaeval census of all, the Domesday Book, are more and more regularly a part of the daily scene. Given the accelerated tempo of political, religious, economic and cultural happenings in this span of three generations, it is understandable that historians have often disagreed radically as they have essayed judgments and generalizations about it. For the study of rapid and uncertain change few better examples can be found than this epoch, which was neither well understood by those who participated in it, nor has it been mastered completely by historians in the past century of intensive study.

On one point, however, in their studies of this epoch there is something close to unanimity among historians. All accept the Concordat ratified by Henry V and the legates of Pope Calixtus II on September 23, 1122, at Worms as marking the resolution of the most crucial phase of the conflict between secular and spiritual authority which, rightly or wrongly, both to contemporaries and modern historians, seems to overshadow most other events of the era. On the other hand, as to when this controversy began, there is little accord. Georges Goyau, a French scholar writing the article on the "Cluniac Movement" in the Encyclopedia of the Social Sciences finds, "The campaign [of reform] which Leo IX, Gregory VII, and in lesser degree other popes of the eleventh century envisaged was essentially an outgrowth of the Cluniac movement [founded at Cluny in France in 910 and widely influential by 1050]." Horace K. Mann, commenting on Cardinal Humbert of Silva Candida's Three Books against Simony written about 1058 writes, "[they] were the opening of the fierce war of investiture which was the predominant note of the Gregorian period." Francesco Cognasso's article in the Enciclopedia Cattolica (1951) sees the investiture struggle as having its beginning with a canon legislated in 1049 at the synod held by Leo IX at Rheims; while Siegfried Rietschl's article in the authoritative Realenzyklopädie für protestantische Theologie und Kirche (1901) while acknowledging larger aspects of the affair, would limit the investiture struggle to the forty-six years beginning with Gregory VII's excommunication of Henry IV in 1076 and ending with the Concordat of Worms. These examples by no means cover the whole range of views on this aspect alone.

If the historians have had some difficulties agreeing on a date for the launching of this period of controversy, the results of the conflict have been assessed with equal divergence of opinion. James Bryce, in his distinguished essay The Holy Roman Empire concludes, "Yet the Papacy remained master of the field." while Z. N. Brooke, in his splendid Raleigh Lecture reads the evidence as showing that, "It was a Pyrrhic victory for the Papacy when the king was left in possesson of the field."

Difficulties which thus beset the historian trying to raise the curtain on the first act of this theatre of history, become so multiplied that by the last act, one's villain is found to be another's hero. But what about the body of the play? Goyau, strongly conditioned by the achievements of the Cluniac movement, sees events as stemming from the efforts of the church to reform and revitalize Christian society: "The success of Cluny in excluding the influence of the laity from the monastic sphere encouraged the papacy to attempt a similar reform among the clergy. The investiture contest waged with the empire, the battle against simony, the struggle to enforce celibacy of the priesthood, were varying aspects of this attempt." The late Augustin Fliche, probably the most acute and learned modern student of the entire reform movement (whose extensive scholarly study of the problem was too long and too detailed to be excerpted satisfactorily for inclusion in this problem), observed in 1929, "It is noteworthy that at Worms [in January 1076] there was no question of lay investiture nor of any complications caused thereby: which proves that at the bottom of the struggle between Priesthood and Empire, there were interests of a more general character and that Henry IV wished above all to resist the pretension of the Holy See to direct lay society according to methods applied to the internal government of the Church." Others have seen in the unfolding action the guiding influence of powerful personalities, the shapers of political and ecclesiastical theory, rather than agents of its impact.

Just this brief survey suggests the divergent judgments of various historians on some of the general points within the period under consideration. But how have these differences come about? In part, the answer is to be found simply in the development of European historical writing and the ancillary developments in methodology. The selection from Henry H. Milman, Dean of St. Paul's, presents the rounded prose of a learned, widely read English clergyman, who, though dependent upon inadequate editions of chronicles and other mediaeval writings, very perceptibly surmounted the Protestant sectarianism of his age to present a clear, straightforward, narrative description of the actors and events of the period with emphasis on the personalities of those involved. The first edition of his *History of Latin Christianity* appeared in 1855.

The century following the appearance of Milman's work saw a tremendous advance in historical knowledge, method, and interpretation. Its first half was dominated by the influential German historical method and philosophy with the names of Theodor Mommsen (1817–1903) and Leopold von Ranke (1795–1886) leading the way. Under this German hegemony the high standards of publication of collections of historical documents, as exemplified by the *Monumenta Germaniae Historica,** were firmly established. On the other hand, however, notwithstanding their determination to present history *wie es eigentlich gewesen*, just as it happened without embellishment or interpretation, students of the mediaeval constitution of Germany seem often to have been overcome by their nationalistic aspirations, and tended to view the preoccupation of the German emperors in their struggle with the mediaeval papacy as having subverted the "natural" development of the German nation. This was the conclusion reached when the dissolution of German imperial power was compared with the "successful" evolution of England and France into unified monarchical feudal states. The selection from James Bryce's *Holy Roman Empire,* first published in 1864, and strongly influenced by contemporary German historical scholarship, illustrates this viewpoint.

As the nineteenth century drew to a close, the scholarly editing and publication of Gregory VII's *Register* [collection of papal letters] and of the *Libelli de Lite* [controversial pamphlets] drew attention to the internal problems of the church and pointed up the theoretical positions of the opposing groups. Two works which appeared about this time and strongly influenced the direction of research for many years were *The Proprietary Church as an Element of Mediaeval Germanic Ecclesiastical Law,* an address delivered at Basel in 1894 by Ulrich Stutz, and the contemporary volumes of E. Sackur *The Cluniacs in Their Ecclesiastical and General Historical Activity to the End of the Eleventh Century.* Stutz's thesis was that the intruding Germanic tribes disrupted the system of canon law and ecclesiastical organization evolved under Roman law as well as the Roman system of governmental organization under which the bishop as the head of his diocese was the keystone to the entire ecclesiastical system and all property (churches, chapels, books, vestments, vessels, and landed property, etc.) was vested in him and placed under his total control. Stutz argued that since the Germanic system recognized no abstract concept of "state" property, and since churches and chapels stood on private lands, only the property of individuals, including their kings and the proprietor and his family, were recognized as having full rights over everything in and of the church except the

---

* *Monumenta Germaniae Historica-Historical Monuments of Germany,* the title of a series of publications of the original Latin documents of the Middle Ages. These volumes contain the laws, treaties, correspondence, poetry, annals and chronicles of or about German history. The publications began in 1819 under the direction of G. H. Pertz and are still appearing. As scholarly technique and knowledge has advanced, the *M.G.H.* has re-edited some of its earlier works. A high standard of research and publication has almost invariably been maintained.

altar. Crudely put, it was understood that the church could be made to yield a maximum profit for the proprietor which usually meant, conversely, a minimum outlay for religion. This attitude toward the church spread throughout France, Spain, and Italy and, after the Carolingian period, moved upward to include even the highest offices of the church. Stutz found that Henry III's appointment of popes derived at least in part from the Emperor's conception of his proprietary rights as Emperor of the Roman Empire. The investiture struggle, therefore, in Stutz's opinion, stemmed from the basic conflict between the old Roman and canon law tradition of episcopal control of the church and its property, and the Germanic tradition under which undefined but generally extensive rights over the church were reserved to the lay proprietor. The ideas of Stutz, developed in many subsequent works, have been tested and criticized by a host of scholars. Many of them have accepted his viewpoint though in modified form. Such a view is reflected in the selection from the American mediaevalist, Catherine F. Boyd, who has examined minutely the question of ownership or the rights to ecclesiastical tithes in northern and central Italy.

The second work, by E. Sachur, on the influence of Cluny, likewise opened up a huge field of inquiry. Stimulated by his approach, a more profound study of monasticism, and especially of its internal development, has led many historians to underline the fact that the ideal of monasticism was the perfection of the individual soul in its search for God, and that although monks and monasteries were reformed to observe strictly the Rule of St. Benedict, it does not necessarily follow that Cluny and the other reformed monastic centers gave any more than moral support to *papal* aspirations. In fact, such a modern authority as Dom David Knowles, O.S.B., takes pains to distinguish clearly between Cluny with its very great emphasis upon elaborate liturgical requirements and, for example, the prominent monastery of Bec in Normandy, which with less emphasis on the service of the altar tended to produce great scholars and administrators like Lanfranc and St. Anselm. Thus, the more carefully monasticism has been studied in all its manifestations throughout western Europe, the less willing are historians to pinpoint any single unitary influence upon secular affairs or attitudes. All are agreed that reformed Benedictine houses exerted influence upon the religious life and attitudes of western Europe, but just how it was exerted, beyond raising the moral level of monks, is too difficult to generalize. The selections from Knowles and Schieffer show how ideas have moved from the position of Sackur on the Cluniac role in this rapidly changing period.

While the works of Stutz and Sackur opened up broad new approaches to the study, new realizations of the problem of the investiture controversy with their studies of proprietary rights and monasticism, others outside the realm of Germanic scholarship were also moving equally vigorously in the editing and publication of mediaeval documents. In France, Léopold Delisle, Louis Duchesne, and Augustin Fliche — to mention only a few within the past eighty years — produced important collections of documents and used them as starting points for new interpretations of the middle ages. For example, Duchesne's edition of the *Liber Pontificalis* [Biographies of the Roman Bishops] opened the way to intensive studies of the papal curia or court and the steps by which it acquired its unique position of authority in Christendom. In turn, Delisle's vast knowledge of palaeography, manuscripts, mediaeval libraries, and cultural monuments over the entire period made him one of the leaders of a great age of French mediaeval scholarship. Fliche, working under the shadow of the great men of this age, devoted a lifetime of teaching and writing to the period of the Gregorian reform. He studied systematically both the major and minor figures as well as the movement of events, uncovering an amazing quantity of unknown manuscript materials in the process. In spite of his heroic effort and the splendid synthesis he offered, his views summarized earlier in this introduction have not swept the field. Other scholars in assessing his work have felt that some currents in the period flowed far stronger than he realized and that many of the personalities had interests far beyond or stronger than those noticed by him.

English, like German and French scholarship, produced a notable group of historians representing several schools of thought. The names of Lord Acton (d. 1902), the planner and first editor of the *Cambridge Modern History,* and Mandell Creighton (d. 1901), the first editor of the *English Historical Review,* along with Bishop Stubbs and F. W. Maitland in constitutional and legal history, are notable as having cleared the ground for fruitful planting in mediaeval studies. Maitland in particular with great discernment pointed to those things peculiar to English development as well as to institutions common to European development. He made the point in the essay *Canon Law in England* [*English Historical Review,* 1901] that the Church of England in the Middle Ages was a constituent part of Latin Christianity and, as such, was bound by the canon law then in vigor. And in 1931, Z. N. Brooke, *The English Church and the Papacy from the Conquest to the Reign of John,* not only confirmed Maitland's earlier argument but even demonstrated clearly that the legal relations between England and Rome were already consolidated as early as the time of Lanfranc of Bec, William the Conqueror's first archbishop of Canterbury.

Inevitably some new areas and new ideas studied by European scholars over the past seventy years have slowly but steadily brought modifications of positions held by earlier generations with a strong political or nationalistic orientation. New studies in the history of mediaeval political theory, the history of law — Roman, canon, and customary — and the history of ideas (*Ideengeschichte*) — the latter closely allied with the history of art and literature —

taken together have shown that the seemingly well-established fact, when examined in every facet and against a background continuously in flux, is subject to a variety of interpretations. In the era of the Gregorian reform phrases such as *Vicar of Christ* and *Anointed by God,* phrases merely symbolic to our ears, had specific and concrete meanings which could be and often were represented artistically in various forms in statuary, miniatures, and frescoes. Geoffrey Barraclough points to the papal party in Germany and Italy as the "revolutionary" party because it claimed the right to depose kings since the *pope* was Vicar of Christ; while the German imperial party knew that Emperor Henry III had deposed popes because the *emperor* was the Vicar of Christ.

Within the period of the investiture controversy is first discernible a slowly growing trend (only realized in the thirteenth century) toward systematic centralization of institutions. The ecclesiastical party increasingly organized and systematized its law and instruments of government not only from the pope down to the parish but likewise in the monastic and religious orders. The operations of the papacy were increasingly centralized in the legal, financial, and administrative spheres, enough to make the trend visible to discriminating eyes in the eleventh century. The significance of the new canonical collections, as clearly pointed out in the works of Paul Fournier, particularly in Gregory VII's own lifetime, was that they set out deliberately to fix all authority, legislative and judicial, in the hierarchy of the Roman church. Gregory's *Dictatus Papae* simply summarized the aims of this centralizing tendency. Within the intellectual construct known as scholasticism, theology and philosophy were also given systematic form. On the secular side, England and France gradually consolidated strong feudal monarchies with a highly developed, practical system for justice. Latin Christianity in its wars at home and abroad slowly developed a centralized system of military organization adequate to the needs of the time. Meanwhile, in the style called Romanesque, the first European-wide art form became visible. What was the relationship, cause, effect, or neither, of this trend to the investiture struggle?

For the historians of the "Investiture Controversy" or "Gregorian Reform" or "Imperial Reaction," there can be no simple answer or naive enumeration of causes and results. As one reads over the views presented in the selections, a few points should be kept in mind to facilitate sorting out the differences as well as the concordances of the writers.

Does the writer have a dynamic conception of the eleventh century? Does he state, assume, or simply neglect the rapid growth of urban life in northern Italy, the lower Rhine valley and at the ends of the Alpine passes? Does the selection make any point of the growth of canon law (slow from the ninth to the early eleventh century; then extremely rapid from about 1050 to 1130)? Is the writer clear on what constitutes monastic reforms and does he indicate concrete evidence relating the Cluniac monasticism with the reforms of the secular church? With the reformed and reforming Papacy? Does he assume that the interests of the great feudal houses, and feudal monarchs were the same throughout western Europe? Was there the same conception of the divine character of rulership in all parts of Europe or was this the inheritance of the Empire alone? Do the writers that discuss international affairs recognize a notable shift in the "power" pattern with the rise of William the Conqueror in England, the establishment of the Norman dynasty in Italy and the virtual withdrawal of Byzantine power from Italy? Does he note the lack of imperial participants in the first Crusade?

Arriving at the central figures of the in-

vestiture struggle and the Italo-German civil wars, what position does the writer take? Is Hildebrand the mastermind of the church reform? Or was he the executive of plans springing from the fertile mind of Humbert of Silva Candida? Was Henry IV the tool of a recognizable power-hungry "gang," or was he a tragic figure attempting to carry on an inherited and outmoded personal policy?

In so far as the various writers included have attempted to assay the meaning of the entire period, what position does each one take? What happened in the period has been variously characterized as constituting revolution; as being merely one phase of the long post-Constantinian struggle between the state and the church to control society; as being guided by a concerted revolutionary effort to establish a theocracy; or, lastly, as the inevitable corollary result of the efforts of the church to regain its rightful form after many generations of deformation at the hands of superior lay power. The student of this period has an obligation to try to decide for himself, after pondering these samples of a century's historiography, which view of the period most nearly accords with historical reality. This is especially important because, as suggested earlier, it was in this era that many of the characteristic features of western civilization received their first formulation. One's answer to the interpretative questions relating to this period will affect necessarily one's view of the broader interpretive issues of European history. Furthermore, however important one may judge it as an historical problem, the basic issue concerning the relationship between church and state remains with us — inescapable and immediate. Or, again, can the world community find a resolution of two ideologies, each one of which, while offering salvation, is based upon antithetical premises?

The Conflict of Opinion

"The age of the investiture controversy may rightly be regarded as the turning-point in medieval civilization. It was the fulfillment of the early Middle Ages because in it the acceptance of the Christian religion by the Germanic peoples reached its final and decisive stage. On the other hand, the greater part of the religious and political system of the high Middle Ages emerged out of the events and ideas of the investiture controversy."

— NORMAN F. CANTOR

"Attention has often been drawn recently to the great contrast between the first reform movements and what we are accustomed to call the Hildebrandine Spirit. The distinction lies chiefly in the fact that before the middle of the eleventh century the reformers concentrated upon the more glaring abuses, with a certain indifference to the means by which this could be effected. . . . But when Hildebrand became Pope in 1073, under the title of Gregory VII, a change was almost at once perceptible, a change to be attributed solely to the powerful personality of one of the most original figures of the Middle Ages. . . . It was Gregory's successors who turned it into a contest about investitures and the right of the monarchs to grant to ecclesiastics the temporal possessions annexed to great churches."

— T. M. PARKER

"Once set free, the Pope [Paschal II] as was natural, disavowed his extorted concessions, and the struggle was protracted for ten years longer, until nearly half a century had elapsed from the first quarrel between Gregory VII and Henry IV. The Concordat of Worms, concluded in A.D. 1122, was in form a compromise, designed to spare either party the humiliation of defeat. Yet the Papacy remained master of the field."

— JAMES BRYCE

"With his [Pope Gregory VII] death in 1085, there is a change of motif. For his successors, while they continually repeated his decree against lay investiture, did not use it for the purpose for which he had intended it. With him it had been the spiritual work of the bishop that mattered, so he had concentrated on the method of appointment; they concentrated on the temporal possessions and services, which he had ignored. . . . When the long schism came to an end, this was the situation with which the new king of Germany was faced. Investiture is now of prime importance, its removal an end in itself, since the other decrees are nugatory without it. Its abolition is therefore the one desideratum with the papal party. But by concentrating upon it they lost their ultimate aim. The king had something with which to barter; by renouncing investiture he gave up the shadow and retained the substance — all that part of the customary procedure which ensured his control over the appointment of bishops and over the bishops when appointed. So Gregory's purpose was defeated when what he intended as a means became an end. It was a Pyrrhic triumph for the Papacy when the king was left in possession of the field."

— ZACHARY N. BROOKE

"Nor were the twin problems of investiture and canonical election, important as they were in practical politics, more than side-issues, significant mainly as the expression of more fundamental divergences. What was at issue was the whole accepted and time-hallowed position of the Salian monarchy. . . . Fundamentally, therefore, the contest between Gregory VII and Henry IV centered round the monarchy and its place in Christian society. It was an issue with the widest ramifications, reaching out into all spheres of social and political life, and in the struggle which ensued the monarchists were the conservative, the Gregorians the revolutionary party."

— GEOFFREY BARRACLOUGH

"The Concordat of Worms, which ended the struggle between Papacy and Empire in 1122, concerned solely the bishoprics and abbacies. The battle against lay proprietorship was essentially won as far as the upper churches were concerned. But the lower churches, namely the parishes and the multitudinous chapels and lesser churches, were left outside the agreements which ended the investiture controversy. The Church had won in essentials the battle against simony and clerical marriage; it had virtually destroyed the Emperor's power over the Church in Italy and had broken the opposition of the Lombard episcopate. But it had not driven the laity from their entrenched position in the rural parishes; and it had not ended the proprietary regime in the lower churches."

— CATHERINE F. BOYD

". . . the temporal ruler performed quasi-episcopal as well as royal offices in the Church; indeed, he was a "pontifical" king, "the head of the Church." Between the "pontifical" king of the Salians and the "royal" pontiff of the reformed Papacy, there was no ground for amicable compromise; and after a struggle of fifty years, they were reconciled only at the cost of the secularization of the imperial office and the irreparable weakening of its administrative power."

— KARL F. MORRISON

LATIN CHRISTIANITY

HENRY HART MILMAN

The selection from Dean Milman's most famous work, *The History of Latin Christianity down to the Death of Pope Nicholas V*, very nicely illustrates the point of view of an eminent, learned, liberal student of ecclesiastical history at the middle of the last century. Henry Hart Milman, born in 1791, graduated from Brasenose College, Oxford, with a B.A. in 1814, and entered holy orders during 1816. He was a recognized classical scholar, poet in the classical languages, and a playwright whose works were performed on the London stage. His edition of Gibbon's *Decline and Fall*, published in 1833, showed his large and accurate knowledge of European history. *Latin Christianity*, first published in 1855, demonstrated his ability to follow the growth and development of a great historic institution in such a manner that one of his critics could attest of the second edition (1856) that "[it] may be said to have permanently raised the standard of ecclesiastical history."

The student should note — while being conscious of the uncritical editions of mediaeval works at the disposal of Dean Milman — the strong emphasis placed upon Gregory VII and the "Hildebrand" reform in this narrative work. The sketch presented of Hildebrand and his struggle with Henry IV should be borne in mind when reading later interpreters.

THE clergy were assembled [April 21, 1073] in the Lateran church to celebrate the obsequies of Alexander; Hildebrand, as Archdeacon, was performing the mournful service. At once from the whole multitude of clergy and people arose a simultaneous cry, "Hildebrand is Pope!" "St. Peter chooses the Archdeacon Hildebrand!" The Archdeacon rushed towards the pulpit to allay the tumult, and either with real or assumed modesty to repel the proffered honour; but Hugo the White, a cardinal presbyter of weight and influence, yet under the accusation of simony and excommunicated by the late Pope, eager perhaps to retrieve his endangered position, at once came forward and made himself heard above the acclamations of the multitude. "Well know ye," he said, "beloved brethren, that since the days of the blessed Leo this tried and prudent Archdeacon has exalted the Roman See, and delivered this city from many perils. Wherefore, since we cannot find any one better qualified for the government of the Church or the protection of the city, we, the bishops and cardinals, with one voice elect him as the pastor and bishop of your souls." The voice of Hugo was drowned in universal cries, "It is the will of St. Peter; Hildebrand is Pope." Hildebrand was led to the Papal throne; he was presented to the people as a man of profound theological knowledge, as a man of prudence, a lover of equity and justice, firm in adversity, temperate in prosperity; according to the Apostolic words, of good conversation; blameless, modest, sober, chaste, hospitable, one that ruleth his own house; a man well brought up in the bosom of his Mother Church, and advanced already for his distinguished merits to the dignity of Archdeacon. "This our Archdeacon then we choose, to be called henceforth and for

Reprinted from Henry Hart Milman, *The History of Latin Christianity down to the Death of Pope Nicholas V*, Vol. III, pp. 479–484; Vol. IV, pp. 11–13, 292–295 (London, 1872).

1

ever by the name of Gregory, for our Pontiff, as the successor of the Apostle." He was immediately arrayed with the scarlet robe, crowned with the Papal tiara, and, reluctant and in tears, enthroned in the chair of St. Peter.

Hildebrand wept! Were they tears of pride and joy, or of humility and sadness, or of mingling and conflicting emotions? It was impossible but that his ambition, his conscious superiority, must long have contemplated this ultimate advancement; but even his firm mind, in its profound religious devotion, may have been shaken at this crisis in his life. The higher Hildebrand estimated the power of the Pope, the more awful the responsibility. According to his view the Pope stood alone on earth between God and man; the destinies of the human race, the temporal no less than the eternal destinies, which must depend on the issue of the imminent contest into which he was about to plunge, hung henceforward upon his acts and words. The monk was not entirely dead within him; to his monastic friends, especially to Desiderius, Abbot of Monte Casino, afterwards his successor, he imparts, with seeming sincerity, the struggle of mind with which he undertook the inevitable office.

He commenced his reign with temper and prudence. The decree of Nicolas II had acknowledged that, in the last instance, after the nomination of the Cardinals, the ratification by the clergy and by the people of Rome, the assent of the Emperor was necessary to complete the full legal title. Gregory despatched messengers to Germany to inform Henry IV of his elevation, and to receive his assent. It is said that at the same time he warned the Emperor not to sanction his nomination; the warning was couched in words of prophetic minacity: "If I be indeed made Pope, I must no longer patiently endure your great and flagrant excesses." But this is probably the language of later admirers of the great theocrat, who would at once invest him in all the terrors which he afterwards assumed. In the decree of Nicolas the assent of the

Emperor had been reduced almost to a form; Gregory was a rigid and punctilious observer of forms, and it was most important that there should be no flaw whatever in his charter, no defect of which his enemies might avail themselves hereafter in his title. But by such language, thus more than usually offensive and contemptuous, Gregory himself raised the form into a reality. The words imputed to him absolutely submitted the validity of his election to the Emperor, and acknowledged the Emperor's power to cancel his promotion. It is utterly irreconcilable with his character, directly at issue with the lofty principles so soon, so firmly, and so haughtily maintained by Hildebrand, to suppose that if the Emperor had refused his assent he would quietly have descended from the Pontifical throne; it was either base hypocrisy, or a perfidious attempt to betray the Emperor at once into hostile proceedings. If it be true — if the address of Gregory was more severe than the ordinary parental admonitions which were wont to form part of the Papal addresses to sovereigns — if more than a grave or tender remonstrance against his personal conduct — Gregory must have been prepared to discharge his conscience with this deliberate defiance, with which he cancelled beforehand any claim upon his gratitude for the assent of the Emperor, and held himself at full liberty to appear as an open adversary of the Empire in defence of the loftiest pretensions of the Papacy. It was presuming, too, somewhat over boldly on the timidity and irresolution of the Emperor and his council. Hildebrand's character was too well known — it had been known for too many years — not to excite apprehensions of his ambitious views in Germany. He was an Italian — a Roman prelate. His austerity would alarm all who were either guilty or under the imputation of simoniacal or incontinent lives; he would have many adversaries even among the better, but not unambitious, German prelates. Henry was in truth strongly urged to annul at once the election. "If he did not at once tame this violent man, on no one would the storm fall so heavily as on himself." Count Eberhard of Nellenberg was sent to Rome to demand of the Romans why they had presumed, contrary to ancient usage, to elect the Pope without previous consultation of the Emperor; if the answer was unsatisfactory, Eberhard was to insist on the abdication of Gregory. But Count Eberhard was received with courteous deference by Gregory, who declared that he had not sought, but that the honour had been forced upon him by the clergy and people. He had, however, deferred, and should defer, his inauguration until he had received the assent of the King. This skilful concession was accepted. Eberhard returned to Germany. Gregory, Bishop of Vercelli, the Chancellor of Italy, was sent to Rome to signify the Imperial assent. Hildebrand thus assumed the Pontifical power unembarrassed by a contested title. Yet the watchful Pope still took every opportunity of asserting indirectly the independence of the Papacy. His name of Gregory VII was a declaration that Gregory VI, whose Pontificate had been annulled by the Imperial authority, was a legitimate Pope.

* * *

The first, the avowed object of Gregory's pontificate, was the absolute independence of the clergy, of the Pope, of the great prelates throughout Latin Christendom, down to the lowest functionary, whose person was to become sacred; that independence under which lurked the undisguised pretension to superiority. His remote and somewhat more indistinct vision, was the foundation of a vast spiritual autocracy in the person of the Pope, who was to rule mankind by the consentient, but subordinate authority of the clergy throughout the world. For this end the clergy were to become still more completely a separate, inviolable caste; their property equally sacred with their persons. Each in his separate sphere, the Pope above all and comprehending all, was to be sovereign arbiter of all disputes; to

hold in his hands the supreme mediation in questions of war and peace; to adjudge contested successions to kingdoms; to be a great feudal lord, to whom other kings became Beneficiaries. His own arms were to be chiefly spiritual, but the temporal power was to be always ready to execute the ecclesiastical behest against the ungodly rebels who might revolt from its authority; nor did the Churchman refuse altogether to use secular weapons, to employ armies in its own name, or even to permit the use of arms to the priesthood.

For this complete isolation of the hierarchy into a peculiar and inviolable caste was first necessary the reformation of the clergy in two most important preliminary matters; the absolute extirpation of the two evils, which the more rigid churchmen had been denouncing for centuries, to the suppression of which Hildebrand had devoted so much of his active energies. The war against simony and against the concubinage of the clergy (for under this ill-sounding name was condemned all connexion, however legalised, with the female sex), must first be carried to a triumphant issue, before the Church could assume its full and uncontested domination.

* * *

These were the terms of this important treaty, which were read to the German nation amid loud applauses, and received as the fundamental principles of the Papal and Imperial rights.

The Emperor gives up to God, to St. Peter, and to the Catholic Church, the right of investiture by the ring and the pastoral staff; he grants to the clergy throughout the Empire the right of free election; he restores to the Church of Rome, to all other churches and nobles, the possessions and feudal sovereignties which have been seized during the wars in his father's time and his own, those in his possession immediately, and he promises his influence to obtain restitution of those not in his possession. He grants peace to the Pope and to all his partisans, and pledges himself to protect whenever he shall be thereto summoned, the Church of Rome in all things.

The Pope grants that all elections of bishops and abbots should take place in the presence of the Emperor or his commissioners only, without bribery and violence, with an appeal in cases of contested elections to the metropolitan and provincial bishops. The bishop elect in Germany was to receive, by the touch of the sceptre, all the temporal rights, principalities, and possessions of the see, excepting those which were held immediately of the See of Rome; and faithfully discharge to the Emperor all duties incident to those principalities. In all other parts of the Empire the royalties were to be granted to the bishop consecrated within six months. The Pope grants peace to the Emperor and his adherents, and promises aid and assistance on all lawful occasions.

The treaty was ratified by the most solemn religious ceremony. The papal legate, the Bishop of Ostia, celebrated the mass, administered the Eucharist to the Emperor, declared him to be reconciled with the Holy See, and received him and all his partisans with the kiss of peace into the bosom of the Catholic Church. The Lateran Council ratified this momentous treaty, which became thereby the law of Christendom.

So closed one period of the long strife between the Church and the Empire. The Christendom of our own calmer times, when these questions, excepting among rigid controversialists, are matters of remote history, may wonder that where the principles of justice, dominant at the time, were so plain and simple, and where such slight and equitable concessions on either side set this long quarrel at rest, Germany should be wasted by civil war, Italy suffer more than one disastrous invasion, one Emperor be reduced to the lowest degradation, more than one Pope be exposed to personal insult and suffering, in short, that such long, bloody, and implacable warfare should lay waste a large part of Europe, on points which admitted such easy adjust-

ment. But, as usual in the collision of great interests, the point in dispute was not the sole, nor even the chief object of the conflict: it was on one part the total independence, and through the independence the complete ascendancy; on the other, if not the absolute subjugation, the secret subservience of the spiritual power; which the more sagacious and ambitious of each party aimed eventually at securing to themselves. Both parties had gradually receded from this remote and unacknowledged purpose, and now contended on open and ostensible ground. The Pope either abandoned as unattainable, or no longer aspired to make the Church absolutely independent both as to election and as to the possession of vast feudal rights without the obligations of feudal obedience to the Empire. In Germany alone the bishops and abbots were sovereign princes of such enormous territorial possessions and exalted rank, that if constant and unswerving subjects and allies of the Pope, they would have kept the Empire in complete subjugation to Rome. But this rival sway had been kept down through the direct influence exercised by the Emperor in the appointment, and his theoretic power at least of withholding the temporalities of the great spiritual fiefs; and the exercise of this power led to monstrous abuses, the secularisation of the Church, the transformation of bishops and abbots to laymen invested in mitres and cowls. The Emperor could not hope to maintain the evils of the old system, the direct appointment of his creatures, boys or rude soldiers, to those great sees or abbacies; or to sell them and receive in payment some of the estates of the Church, and so to create an unconstitutional and independent revenue. It was even a wiser policy, as concerned his temporal interests, to elevate the order in that decent and imposing character which belonged to their sacred calling — to Teutonise the Teutonic hierarchy.

Indirect influence through the chapters might raise up, if a more free and more respected, yet more loyal race of churchmen; if more independent of the Empire they would likewise be more independent of the Pope; they would be Germans as well as churchmen; become not the sworn, immitigable enemies, but the allies, the bulwarks of the Imperial power. So in the subsequent contest the armies of the Hohenstaufen, at least of Frederick Barbarossa, appear commanded by the great prelates of the Empire; and even Frederick II, if he had been more of a German, less of an Italian sovereign, might, supported by the German hierarchy, have maintained the contest with greater hopes of success.

THE HOLY ROMAN EMPIRE

JAMES BRYCE

James Bryce (1838–1922), later honored as Viscount Bryce, was a distinguished classicist, professor of law, member of both houses of Parliament,
ambassador, statesman, and prolific writer. Born in Belfast, Ireland, his father
moved to Glasgow, Scotland, where Bryce entered the University. Later, he
won a scholarship to Trinity College, Oxford, where he had a brilliant undergraduate career in classics and history. He then turned to the law, going to
Heidelberg for further study. It is often pointed out that the *Holy Roman
Empire* was the winner of the Arnold Historical Prize for 1863, but it should
be kept in mind that this famous work was by modern standards far above the
level of an undergraduate prize essay.

While Bryce's interpretation still lays great weight upon a "Hildebrandine
program," there is no doubt about his understanding of the significance of the
shifts in political power in the period from the death of Henry III to Henry V.
Brilliant strokes on a large canvas fairly describe Bryce's style and the vigor
which made this book widely read in 1864, still carries forward the reader
nearly a century later.

UNDER Conrad's son, Henry III, the Empire attained the meridian of its power. At home Otto the Great's prerogative had not stood so high. The duchies, always the chief source of fear, were allowed to remain vacant or filled by the relatives of the monarch, who himself retained, contrary to usual practice, those of Franconia and (for some years) Swabia. Abbeys and sees lay entirely in his gift. Intestine feuds were repressed by the proclamation of a public peace. Abroad, the feudal superiority over Hungary, which Henry II had gained by conferring the title of king with the hand of his sister Gisela, was enforced by war, the country made almost a province, and compelled to pay tribute. In Rome no German sovereign had ever been so absolute. A disgraceful contest between three claimants of the papal chair had shocked even the reckless apathy of Italy. Henry deposed them all and appointed their successor: he became hereditary patrician, and wore constantly the green mantle and circlet of gold which were the badges of that office, seeming, one might think, to find in it some further authority than that which the imperial name conferred. The synod passed a decree granting to Henry the right of nominating the supreme pontiff; and the Roman priesthood, who had forfeited the respect of the world even more by habitual simony than by the flagrant corruption of their manners, were forced to receive German after German as their bishop, at the bidding of a ruler so powerful, so severe and so pious. But Henry's encroachments alarmed his own nobles no less than the Italians, and the reaction, which might have been dangerous to himself, was fatal to his successor. A mere chance, as some might call it, determined the course of history. The great Emperor died suddenly in A.D. 1056,

Reprinted from James Bryce, *The Holy Roman Empire*, pp. 147–159 (New York, 1886).

and a child was left at the helm, while storms were gathering that might have demanded the wisest hand.

Reformed by the Emperors and their Teutonic nominees, the papacy had resumed in the middle of the eleventh century the schemes of polity shadowed forth by Nicholas I, and which the degradation of the last age had only suspended. Under the guidance of her greatest mind, Hildebrand, the archdeacon of Rome, she now advanced to their completion, and proclaimed that war of ecclesiastical power against the civil power in the person of the Emperor, which became the center of the subsequent history of both. While the nature of the struggle cannot be understood without a glance at their previous connection, the vastness of the subject warns one from the attempt to draw even its outlines, and restricts our view to those relations of Popedom and Empire which arise directly out of their respective positions as heads spiritual and temporal of the universal Christian state.

The eagerness of Christianity in the age immediately following her political establishment to purchase by submission the support of the civil power, has been already remarked. The change from independence to supremacy was gradual. The tale we smile at, how Constantine, healed of his leprosy, granted the West to Bishop Sylvester, and retired to Byzantium that no secular prince might interfere with the jurisdiction or profane the neighborhood of Peter's chair, worked great effects through the belief it commanded for many centuries. Nay more, its groundwork was true. It was the removal of the seat of government from the Tiber to the Bosphorus that made the Pope the greatest personage in the city, and in the prostration after Alaric's invasion he was seen to be so. Henceforth he alone was a permanent and effective, though still unacknowledged power, as truly superior to the revived senate and consuls of the phantom republic as Augustus and Tiberius had been to the

faint continuance of their earlier prototypes. Pope Leo the First asserted the universal jurisdiction of his see, and his persevering successors slowly enthralled Italy, Illyricum, Gaul, Spain, Africa, dexterously confounding their undoubted metropolitan and patriarchal rights with those of œcumenical bishop, in which they were finally merged. By his writings and the fame of his personal sanctity, by the conversion of England and the introduction of an impressive ritual, Gregory the Great did more than any other pontiff to advance Rome's ecclesiastical authority. Yet his tone to Maurice of Constantinople was deferential, to Phocas adulatory; his successors were not consecrated till confirmed by the Emperor or the Exarch; one of them was dragged in chains to the Bosphorus, and banished thence to Scythia. When the iconoclastic controversy and the intervention of Pipin broke the allegiance of the Popes to the East, the Franks, as patricians and Emperors, seemed to step into the position which Byzantium had lost. . . . Their relations were, however, no longer the same. If the Frank vaunted conquest, the priest spoke only of free gift. What Christendom saw was that Charles was crowned by the Pope's hands, and undertook as his principal duty the protection and advancement of the Holy Roman Church. The circumstances of Otto the Great's coronation gave an even more favorable opening to sacerdotal claims, for it was a Pope who summoned him to Rome and a Pope who received from him an oath of fidelity and aid. In the conflict of three powers, the Emperor, the Pontiff and the people — represented by their senate and consuls, or by the demagogue of the hour — the most steady, prudent and farsighted was sure eventually to prevail. The Popedom had no minorities, as yet few disputed successions, few revolts within its own army — the host of churchmen through Europe. Boniface's conversion of Germany under its direct sanction, gave it a hold on the rising hierarchy of the greatest European state; the extension of the rule of Charles and Otto diffused in the same measure its emissaries and pretensions. The first disputes turned on the right of the prince to confirm the elected Pontiff, which was afterward supposed to have been granted by Hadrian I to Charles, in the decree quoted as *"Hadrianus Papa."* This *"ius eligendi et ordinandi summum pontificem,"* [right of electing and ordaining the sovereign pontiff] which Lewis I appears as yielding by the *"Ego Ludovicus,"* was claimed by the Carolingians whenever they felt themselves strong enough, and having fallen into desuetude in the troublous times of the Italian Emperors, was formally renewed to Otto the Great by his nominee Leo VIII. We have seen it used, and used in the purest spirit, by Otto himself, by his grandson Otto III, last of all, and most despotically by Henry III. Along with it there had grown up a bold counter-assumption of the Papal chair to be itself the source of the imperial dignity. In submitting to a fresh coronation, Lewis the Pious admitted the invalidity of his former self-performed one: Charles the Bald did not scout the arrogant declaration of John VIII, that to him alone the Emperor owed his crown; and the council of Pavia, when it chose him King of Italy, repeated the assertion. Subsequent Popes knew better than to apply to the chiefs of Saxon and Franconian chivalry language which the feeble Nuestrian had not resented; but the precedent remained, the weapon was only hid behind the pontifical robe to be flashed out with effect when the moment should come. There were also two other great steps which Papal power had taken. By the invention and adoption of the False Decretals[1] it had provided itself with a legal system suited to any emergency, and which gave it unlimited authority through the Christian world in causes spiritual and over persons ecclesiastical. Canonistical ingenuity found it easy in one way or another to make this include all causes and persons whatsover: for crime is always and wrong is often sin, nor can aught be anywhere done which may not affect the clergy. On the gift of Pipin and Charles, repeated and confirmed by Lewis I, Charles II, Otto I and III, and now made to rest on the more venerable authority of the first Christian Emperor, it could found claims to the sovereignty of Rome, Tuscany and all else that had belonged to the exarchate. Indefinite in their terms, these grants were never meant by the donors to convey full dominion over the districts that belonged to the head of the Empire — but only as in the case of other church estates, a sort of perpetual usufruct, a beneficial enjoyment which had nothing to do with sovereignty. They were, in fact, mere endowments. Nor had the gifts been ever actually reduced into possession; the Pope had been hitherto the victim, not the lord of the neighboring barons. They were not, however, denied, and might be made a formidable engine of attack; appealing to them, the Pope could brand his opponents as unjust and impious; and could summon nobles and cities to defend him as their liege lord, just as, with no better original right, he invoked the help of the Norman conquerors of Naples and Sicily.

The attitude of the Roman Church to the imperial power at Henry III's death was externally respectful. The right of a German king to the crown of the city was undoubted, and the Pope was his lawful subject. Hitherto the initiative in reform had come from the civil magistrate. But the secret of the pontiff's strength lay in this: he, and he alone, could confer the crown, and had therefore the right of imposing conditions on the recipient. Frequent interregna had weakened the claim of the Transalpine monarch and prevented his power from taking firm root; his title was never by law hereditary: the holy Church had before sought and might again seek a defender elsewhere. And since the need of such defence had originated this transference of the Empire from the Greeks to the Franks, since to render it was the

---

[1] A large collection of canon law containing many forged and interpolated texts, which began to circulate in France about 840. [Editor's note.]

Emperor's chief function, it was surely the Pope's duty as well as his right to see that the candidate was capable of fulfilling his task, to degrade him if he rejected or misperformed it.

The first step was to remove a blemish in the constitution of the Church, by fixing a regular body to choose the supreme pontiff. This Nicholas II did in A.D. 1059, feebly reserving the rights of Henry IV and his successors. Then the reforming spirit, kindled by the abuses and depravity of the last century, advanced apace. It had two main objects — the enforcement of celibacy, especially on the secular clergy, who enjoyed in this respect considerable freedom; and the extinction of simony. In the former, the Emperors and a large part of the laity were not unwilling to join: the latter no one dared to defend in theory. But when Gregory VII declared that it was sin for the ecclesiastic to receive his benefice under conditions from a layman, and so condemned the whole system of feudal investitures to the clergy, he aimed a deadly blow at all secular authority. Half of the land and wealth of Germany was in the hands of bishops and abbots, who would now be freed from the monarch's control to pass under that of the Pope. In such a state of things government itself would be impossible.

Henry and Gregory already mistrusted each other: after this decree war was inevitable. The Pope cited his opponent to appear and be judged at Rome for his vices and misgovernment. The Emperor replied by convoking a synod, which deposed and insulted Gregory. At once the dauntless monk pronounced Henry excommunicate, and fixed a day on which, if still unrepentant, he should cease to reign. Supported by his own princes, the monarch might have defied a command backed by no external force; but the Saxons, never contented since the first place had passed from their own dukes to the Franconians, only waited the signal to burst into a new revolt, while through all Germany the Emperor's tyranny and irregularities of life had sown the seeds of disaffection. Shunned, betrayed, threatened, he rushed into what seemed the only course left, and Canossa saw Europe's mightiest prince, titular lord of the world, a suppliant before the successor of the Apostle. Henry soon found that his humiliation had not served him; driven back into opposition, he defied Gregory anew, set up an anti-pope, overthrew the rival whom his rebellious subjects had raised, and maintained to the end of his sad and checkered life a power often depressed but never destroyed. Nevertheless had all other humiliation been spared, that one scene in the yard of the Countess Matilda's castle, an imperial penitent standing barefoot and woolen-frocked on the snow three days and nights, till the priest who sat within should admit and absolve him, was enough to mark a decisive change, and inflict an irretrievable disgrace on the crown so abased. Its wearer could no more, with the same lofty confidence, claim to be the highest power on earth, created by and answerable to God alone. Gregory had extorted the recognition of that absolute superiority of the spiritual dominion which he was wont to assert so sternly; proclaiming that to the Pope, as God's Vicar, all mankind are subject, and all rulers responsible: so that he, the giver of the crown, may also excommunicate and depose. Writing to William the Conqueror, he says: "For as for the beauty of this world, that it may be at different seasons perceived by fleshly eyes, God hath disposed the sun and the moon, lights that outshine all others; so lest the creature whom His goodness hath formed after His own image in this world should be drawn astray into fatal dangers, He hath provided in the apostolic and royal dignities the means of ruling it through divers offices. . . . If I, therefore, am to answer for thee on the dreadful day of judgment before the just Judge who cannot lie, the creator of every creature, bethink thee whether I must not very diligently provide for thy salvation, and whether, for thine own safety, thou oughtest not without delay to obey me, that so thou mayest possess the land of the living."

Gregory was not the inventor nor the first propounder of these doctrines; they had been long before a part of mediaeval Christianity, interwoven with its most vital doctrines. But he was the first who dared to apply them to the world as he found it. His was that rarest and grandest of gifts, an intellectual courage and power of imaginative belief which, when it has convinced itself of aught, accepts it fully with all its consequences, and shrinks not from acting at once upon it. A perilous gift, as the melancholy end of his own career proved, for men were found less ready than he had thought them to follow out with unswerving consistency like his the principles which all acknowledged. But it was the very suddenness and boldness of his policy that secured the ultimate triumph of his cause, awing men's minds and making that seem realized which had been till then a vague theory. His premises once admitted — and no one dreamed of denying them — the reasonings by which he established the superiority of spiritual to temporal jurisdiction were unassailable. With his authority, in whose hands are the keys of heaven and hell, whose word can bestow eternal bliss or plunge in everlasting misery, no other earthly authority can compete or interfere: if his power extends into the infinite, how much more must he be supreme over things finite? It was thus that Gregory and his successors were wont to argue: the wonder is, not that they were obeyed, but that they were not obeyed more implicitly. In the second sentence of excommunication which Gregory passed upon Henry IV are these words:

"Come now, I beseech you, O most holy and blessed Fathers and Princes, Peter and Paul, that all the world may understand and know that if ye are able to bind and to loose in heaven, ye are likewise able on earth, according to the merits of each man, to give and to take away empires, kingdoms, princedoms, marquisates, duchies, countships and the possessions of all men. For if ye judge spiritual things, what must we believe to be your power over worldly thing? and if ye judge the angels who rule over all proud princes, what can ye not do to their slaves?"

Doctrines such as these do indeed strike equally at all temporal governments, nor were the Innocents and Bonifaces of later days slow to apply them so. On the Empire, however, the blow fell first and heaviest. As when Alaric entered Rome, the spell of ages was broken, Christendom saw her greatest and most venerable institution dishonored and helpless; allegiance was no longer undivided, for who could presume to fix in each case the limits of the civil and ecclesiastical jurisdictions. The potentates of Europe beheld in the Papacy a force which, if dangerous to themselves, could be made to repel the pretensions and baffle the designs of the strongest and haughtiest among them. Italy learned how to meet the Teutonic conqueror by gaining the papal sanction for the leagues of her cities. The German princes, anxious to narrow the prerogative of their head, were the natural allies of his enemy, whose spiritual thunders, more terrible than their own lances, could enable them to depose an aspiring monarch, or extort from him any concessions they desired. Their altered tone is marked by the promise they required from Rudolf of Swabia, whom they set up as a rival to Henry, that he would not endeavor to make the throne hereditary.

It is not possible here to dwell on the details of the great struggle of the Investitures, rich as it is in the interest of adventure and character, momentous as were its results for the future. A word or two must suffice to describe the conclusion, not indeed of the whole drama, which was to extend over centuries, but of what may be called its first act. Even that act lasted beyond the lives of the original performers. Gregory VII passed away at Salerno in A.D. 1085, exclaiming with his last breath, "I have loved justice and hated iniquity, therefore I die in exile." Twenty-one years later, in A.D. 1106, Henry IV died, dethroned by an unnatural son whom the hatred of a relentless pontiff had raised in rebellion against him. But that son, the Emperor Henry V, so far from conceding the points in dispute, proved an antagonist more ruthless and not less able than his father. He claimed for his crown all the rights over ecclesiastics that his predecessors had ever enjoyed, and when at his coronation in Rome, A.D. 1111, Pope Paschal II refused to complete the rite until he should have yielded, Henry seized both Pope and cardinals and compelled them by a rigorous imprisonment to consent to a treaty which he dictated. Once set free, the Pope, as was natural, disavowed his extorted concessions, and the struggle was protracted for ten years longer, until nearly half a century had elapsed from the first quarrel between Gregory VII and Henry IV. The Concordat of Worms, concluded in A.D. 1122, was in form a compromise, designed to spare either party the humiliation of defeat. Yet the Papacy remained master of the field. The Emperor retained but one-half of those rights of investiture which had formerly been his. He could never resume the position of Henry III; his wishes or intrigues might influence the proceedings of a chapter, his oath bound him from open interference. He had entered the strife in the fullness of dignity; he came out of it with tarnished glory and shattered power. His wars had been hitherto carried on with foreign foes, or at worst with a single rebel noble; now his former ally was turned into his fiercest assailant, and had enlisted against him half his court, half the magnates of his realm. At any moment his scepter might be shivered in his hand by the bolt of anathema, and a host of enemies spring up from every convent and cathedral.

THE INFLUENCE OF
THE CLUNIAC MOVEMENT

ERNST SACKUR

Ernst Sackur (1862–1901), the conclusions of whose famous work on the Cluniacs appear here, died at the age of thirty-nine while a professor at the University of Strasbourg. At the time of his death, the author had collected a large amount of material for a full-scale history of Rome to 1300. His work was solidly grounded in the sources of Cluniac history and has strongly influenced all serious historians of monasticism. The student of the investiture movement needs to pay close attention to the geographical spread of "Clunydom," and to its limited monastic aims to the epoch of Leo IX and Henry III.

THE monastery of Cluny was founded and endowed by William the Pious at a time when the spirit of religion everywhere manifested itself against the shattered state of all morality. Contemporaneously, many monasteries had already been re-established or were soon to be founded. If Cluny managed to achieve a dominant position over all other monasteries, it owed this importance, for one thing, to its close contact with the Roman papacy, but, above all, to the personality of its first abbot, Odo. He raised the general reform of monasteries to a principle; he made Rome grant him the right to receive monks of disorganized monasteries and to unite under his leadership several abbeys. His talent for stirring up others and the tenacious will with which Odo pursued this idea secured success for him and created for his successors a foundation on which they could build. In doing this, Odo did not proceed pedantically; it was of primary importance to re-establish communal life; and as far as details were concerned, allowances could certainly be made.

But from the time of the founding of Cluny, it was two decades before Odo could undertake the reform of monasteries on a large scale. The main thing was that (beside the Pope) the rulers were won as well as the founder's family and its vassals, the Burgundian nobility, Rudolf of France, Hugh the Black, Hugh of Franconia. In Italy, Odo had Alberic and Leo VII on his side since they were obligated to him because of his interventions with King Hugh.

In the highest circles the necessity of supporting the Church had again come alive. If these took the lead, the vassals and the people would follow. Slowly at first, then with ever increasing speed the number of donations grew and the property multiplied. Whoever held former Church property was induced to return it.

*　　*　　*

By the beginning of the eleventh century there already existed a large number of reform centers apart from Cluny: Fleury, St. Bénigne of Dijon, St. Julien of Tours. In Lorraine, Richard of Vannes opened a new reform center. Everybody worked in certain areas and dioceses and enjoyed close association with a particular patron. All over France one monastery after another

E. Sackur, *Die Cluniacenser in ihrer kirchlichen und allgemeingeschichtlichen Wirksamkeit bis zur Mitte des elften Jahrhunderts*, Halle, 1892–1894, 2 vol. [Translated by the editor of this volume.]

13

was won in this way to strict discipline, from the regions around the mouth of the Rhone to Brittany in the northwest; in Lorraine and Flanders the reform reached out from the diocese of Verdun to the lowlands of the North Sea.

The main monastery of this reform, the source from which monastic life flowed to the other monasteries was without question Cluny which went back to Benedict of Aniane's institutions; only in Lorraine and on the Somme in the tenth century had the urge of flight from the world led independently to a union and a common life according to the Benedictine Rule. But certainly France, by these spontaneous foundations, did not remain untouched. Also in Italy, the re-awakening religious spirit sought for a new conforming expression. Here, the hermitical life found many adherents. On the other hand, in the upper Italian dioceses the bishops had returned once more to the Benedictine Rule.

If one follows the history of an individual monastery, it cannot possibly be assumed that any single tendency was strongly isolated from the others of that time. Monks of different origin, abbots from different schools often were active in a parallel and successive way. Centralization was probably attempted here and there, and was in some small measure accomplished. Especially at the beginning, the majority of the monasteries received abbots and monks from the mother house, but after that, any connection was severed. Odilo was the first consciously to unite the reformed abbeys in a closer bond to their mother monastery.

At first the reform was carried out in complete freedom; the reformers were content when the main abuses, such as the possession of private property and the eating of meat, were corrected; in minor things they were apparently lenient. This guaranteed success on a broad scale initially, but certainly hindered a constant growth. In most cases the abbots were independent; after their death the brothers had the right of free election of an abbot. The layman,

lord of the castle, and feudal lord, too, might gain influence again, and a generation later one had sometimes to start the Sisyphean labor all over again. Especially in the beginning was this the case in many instances, as the individual monasteries could not draw sufficient support within their own dioceses; soon they had to give way before local powers. To an increasing degree conditions then became fixed. In the tightly woven net the individual members were held closer than by the loose ties at the beginning. But there was no question of a complete security. In Lorraine and on the right bank of the Rhine all signs are that the reforms of Poppo of Stablo were attempted in vain. Occasional orders were given and some intervention took place, but the outcome was never certain.

If this description is correct, then it follows that one cannot use "Cluny-dom" in the sense of the term encompassing all institutions that were once influenced by Cluny. If one sees the Cluniac abbot, Rudolph Glaber, denying the Pope the right to perform clerical ceremonies against the will of the bishop to whom the diocese belonged at the same time that Fleury and Cluny were fighting in support of this right, or when the good Cluniac, Poppo of Stablo, stands up for an uncanonical marriage to which his brother Cluniac, Sigfried of Gorze, was decidedly opposed, it becomes obvious that even in questions of principle there was a lack of general agreement. However, there is no doubt that the leaders of this movement considered themselves as united, that Odilo worked together with William of Dijon as well as with Abbo of Fleury, and that they stood for the same ideas and were agreed also on basic matters.

One may still raise the question in what respect Cluny-dom — for reasons of brevity we are going to use this term to refer to the community of leaders of French monasticism — stood for uniform points of view and to what extent these viewpoints were particularly characteristic of this direction of the movement.

* * *

It is agreed that the Church's historical development as it took place after the fall of the Carolingian empire, reached its zenith in the personality and ideas of Gregory VII. Therefore, whoever describes ecclesiastical tendencies of the tenth and eleventh centuries in a larger context has to emphasize the relation of these ecclesiastical tendencies towards the aspirations of this pope; and anyone who discusses a reform movement like the Cluniac movement out of which Gregory is supposed to have come, has to show especially to what degree these tendencies were in accord with those of Hildebrand, went beyond them, or how far they even contradicted them.

Three main threads can be recognized in Gregory's activity: the idea of a universal church directed by Rome; the idea of the superiority of everything spiritual over everything temporal; the idea of a clergy free from all vices and devoting itself completely to the service of the church: ideas that were by no means new, but which, brought into a system and consequently put into practice would also have a revolutionary effect in other times. What importance did the Cluniac reform movement have for the development of these ideas?

The Roman universal power had developed from the position of honor granted to the Bishop of Rome (the old capital city of the world), and from the asserted claim to enter, as the Apostle's successor, into the rights of St. Peter. But for several centuries this universal power had been a claim rather than an acquired right. It had always brought its influence to bear in so far as the individuality of the wearer of the tiara and the material means which he had at his disposal, advanced the claim of supremacy over all other churches. Since Pippin and Charlemagne, the papacy was the recognized third political world power besides the eastern Roman empire and the western Roman empire renewed by Charlemagne. With its emancipation from Byzantium, the claims of Rome had mounted

sharply. These claims were furthered by the weakness of any central secular power in the west, and the consequent necessity of looking to the pope for protection instead of to the king, and by the need to maintain the unity of the church during the decline of the Frankish empire. But when, about the turn of the ninth century, the papacy could not maintain its political independence, since the pope was forced into the position of an unimportant local bishop by the power of the local Roman nobility, and when the papal dignity became a sinecure held by individual Roman families (for some time hereditary), then under these circumstances there was left little reality of the power of a Nicholas or the sweeping claims of the *False Decretals*. Only now and then did one still seem to remember the Roman bishop: he probably continued to fulfill at least his purely clerical functions, but the great political upheavals were accomplished without his participation. The Italian policy of the Ottonians helped to bring once more the Papacy into immediate touch with great world politics and its actors, but in the long run it was not able to save the Roman See from the power of the nobility and even less was it able to provide qualified princes of the church. It was the frivolity and greed of the gilded youth of Rome that exploited the apostolic throne.

Under these circumstances the bishops and particularly the metropolitans of the various individual regions had gained a nearly independent position. They did not challenge in any way the Pope's supremacy over the church, including the highest judicial functions, or the right of loosing and binding. Theoretically the Roman See's privileges were indisputable for them. But, for one thing, they wanted to make their effective exercise dependent upon the worthiness of the bearer of this power; furthermore, the episcopate tried to establish the principle that the Pope had no right to interfere arbitrarily in the rights of other bishops in their dioceses. Also, they demanded that the ecclesiastical penal authority at the local level should not be breached arbitrarily by the Pope because it would harm discipline. If the Pope was, according to Pseudo-Isidore's theory, the source of all law, then the pyramid of the hierarchy, according to the opinion of his opponents, rested on the broad basis of Episcopal power.

It cannot be denied that even the theoretical recognition of Papal authority was generally obstructed by the clergy and enfeebled in practice, and that the metropolitans ruled churches that were quite independent of Rome. The unimportant rights of confirmation that were granted to Rome and the theoretical recognition of its leadership certainly had little more than honorary value if one took issue with the Pope on every occasion where he asserted his own will. As independently as the national churches seemed to move and to develop, the necessary energies were not lacking which gradually undermined the firm basis of the Episcopal power and which promoted the Roman influence outside of Italy in increasing measure, and which also during the times of the decline of papal power directed everything towards the capital of Christianity.

In this regard the development of French monasticism, in the form of the Cluniac movement, was of great importance. For the monks, representatives of religion, Rome, as the city of the Apostle, always had a claim to pious veneration. They visited the holy places for the grace of prayer and they ascribed to these pilgrimages a high value for the salvation of souls. All the distinguished abbots of that time undertook such journeys from religious motives, but even if they visited Rome for other considerations, still they did not fail to pray at the sacred places. Nobody who claimed to be pious was allowed to miss going to Rome, and for a biographer it was nearly impossible to invite admiration for his hero, if he could not give a report of a pilgrimage to Rome. Laymen also went, and since Gerald of Aurillac had gained admiration and honor through his many Roman journeys (usually as a pilgrim), William V of Acquitaine went nearly every year, likewise to gain status. This all was due to the influence of the monks and therefore they were not pleased at all, when the pilgrimages to the Holy Land began to replace those to Rome.

Being religiously convinced of the succession of Peter, the monks, furthermore, held to the view ascribing to Rome the power of loosing and binding and therewith founded the universal domination of the Roman church. For Abbo of Fleury, Rome was the apex of the Church and the Roman decrees were binding on the entire hierarchy. In the disputes of the abbots of Fleury with the bishops of Orléans, or of those of Cluny with the bishop of Mâcon, in the controversy between William of Dijon and John XIX, when he was about to renounce the title *universalis* in favor of Eastern Rome, again and again the opinion of Cluny is expressed that the right to bind and to loose lies in the power of Peter, and that all rules made in the name of the Pope were to be accepted without comment.

This conception of the universal power of Rome then brought into effectiveness the many-faceted protective relationship with Rome under which Cluny and other greater reform monasteries stood. The French abbots asked continually for Roman protection when bishops or laymen infringed upon their rights and their freedom. With all their energy they took a position supporting the validity of all papal decrees with respect to the episcopate and thereby caused a discussion which resulted always in an advantage for the Apostolic See. In these fights Rome protected them and they defended the universal rights of Rome, which they had to undertake to protect the independence of their institutions: thus was the bond forged which bound them to the bearers of the Apostolic power.

As monasticism had the greatest interest in the power position of the Roman papacy, it is understandable why it followed with interest a policy that tried to free the Roman See from local lay forces and raise it to a higher importance. Since the intervention of Otto I in favor of John XIII, the Cluniac abbots followed with approbation every similar step of the German emperors. They were present when Gregory V replaced John XV, they did not fail to be present when Benedict VIII had to be protected against the Crescenti, and they welcomed the acts of Henry III with unconcealed joy. Any canonical doubts concerning the participation of temporal princes were out of the question, just as there was little question of specific reforms; only that the Roman Pope be approachable to them and independent of the authorities who at will elevated and toppled bishops, instigated street brawls of the towns and robbed the pilgrims to Rome.

In this consisted their entire policy towards Rome. The idea of a universal Church with Rome at the apex was due to a religious point of view. Practical needs led them to claim this idea publicly and to defend the validity of all papal decrees. The wish to have popes who would be able to give them the requisite protection led to supporting a policy such as the German emperors up to that time pursued.

It is obvious that herein lies an understandable development, but no system. The papal decrees had universal validity — but what would happen when the Popes turned the decrees against their protectors, the emperors? It is very interesting to see how the legal system of Abbo of Fleury shows the same unresolved contradiction. According to him the papal decrees have validity for the whole church. On the other hand, the king is master over all his subjects, including also the bishops who have to obey him: his commands are valid also for the church within his empire. This lack of sharp definition of the legal sphere of both powers was on the whole the characteristic point in the ecclesiastical political viewpoint of the Cluniacs. This proves how far they were removed from canonists like Wazo and Hildebrand. Cluny-dom was fighting from a religious basis without sharply defined comprehension of the

vague notion of a peaceful common cause of both powers. It needed the temporal power too much to develop ideas which aimed at complete emancipation from it. The starting points of the monks are notions, that in their further development did not lead to Gregory VII, but to his opponents, Hugo of Fleury and Sigebert of Gembloux. Just as the opinion of Abbo of Fleury had betrayed a strong preference for royal authority, so also Hugh of St. Maria and Sigebert, who grew up in monasteries influenced by Cluny, stood under the spell of the royal point of view. In Cluny friendly faces watched Hildebrand ascend the Roman throne.

* * *

We have only quite briefly to explain wherein the real meaning of the French monastic reform lay.

Cluny-dom did not appear with a program: it was born of a particular world-picture. It had no other intention than that of recalling to life, against a crude materialism of the time, those institutions that permitted an existence in accord with evangelical rules in an unruly society. They were cooperative, autonomous formations such as tend to form in disorganized states under a weak central authority and by means of self-help, supplement the great communities such as State and Church. From this viewpoint stemmed the aim of influencing the neighborhood, to win it over to religion. As the number of reconstructed monasteries increased, the task became greater and greater, but it did not change. The intrinsic purpose had been and remained that of capturing souls. The relations were enlarged; we have seen how the princes were ready to support the efforts of the monks. Very soon every family had its family monastery. Monasticism repaid this concern by trying everywhere to settle strife, to prevent wars, to arrange peace and to protect threatened people from their attackers. It took an active part in the conclusion of peace. It went to the courts. It knew how to make itself agreeable through political services, for which because of their far-reaching connections monks were well qualified, and it also found protection against those who threatened its freedom of action and its privileges.

Through its extraordinary social effectiveness monasticism won the masses. The large, daily growing landed property opened a secure existence to an economically worn-out population. The mobile capital which the monasteries gathered, granted to the economically wavering a support that the monasteries liked to offer. Stately basilicas with marble pillars and stone vaults attracted the mass in need of charity, to whom the splendor of gold and silver altar vessels indicated the power of the saints. Rough warriors wrapped themselves in the mantle of humility, proud feudal lords exchanged the sword for the cross of Christ, and rough farmers listened to the joyful message and acquired more gentle habits. Many bishops, especially in the south, were carried away with enthusiasm, and friends of the movement got bishops' posts. It was a spiritual change that followed: to the sorrow of those who had built hitherto their house on the Carolingian social order; and to the anger, especially, of an episcopate which viewed with fright how monasticism demanded back property which the bishop's church had taken illegally, and how it used in complete independence all religious power for its own purpose; and, finally, how it emancipated the laity from the episcopal oppression, to the advantage of a nearly forgotten central power; and to the annoyance of a secularized temporal clergy who had to renounce their women, their salaries, and the luxurious comfort of a free elegant life without scruples of conscience.

In that way the contrast was also established. The ascetic Roman stream that started in the South finally overpowered the French North, won the new kingdom of the Capetians, and found itself here face to face with an episcopate that struggled desperately against the attack of monasticism, that started from the idea of an all-egalitarian world-philosophy, from the idea of universal Romanism, and that did not have any understanding of the independent pride of a national ecclesiastical church order.

The complete disorder of the French church, and the counter-action of innumerable single forces independent of each other, promoted in the west Frank empire the advancement of that movement to the same degree that the stern organisation of the German imperial Church, with its close connection with royal authority and the morality of the clergy still held them back from the German borders. Only the ecclesiastical-political dissolution that occurred under Henry IV, opened gaps through which the monastic-Roman spirit could penetrate into the German state organism. Appearances like Siegfried of Mainz, who thought out the plan to retire to Cluny, and Anno of Cologne who brought monks from Fruttaria to Lorraine monasteries and with this act gave an example to other bishops — both were, at the first assault of Rome, inclined to give up the dignity of the Empire. Such occurrences were only possible when the bond between the old Church and the Kingdom loosened, when Henry III out of an unhappy personal inclination and deserted by the national episcopate, had made himself dependent on points of view similar to those that had originated in the clergy of the Romance countries. But in the epoch that we have considered, everything was still in twilight. While on the other side of the Vosges mountains the king, the princes, and a great part of the bishops already wore monastic chains, and while the north French episcopate fought a fierce battle against Rome and its militia, the Lorraine bishops probably had found an occasion in the empire to put the guidance and reform of their monasteries into the hands of personal friends, who maintained a distant relationship with Cluny. But Lorraine monastic life neither could establish itself on the other side of the Rhine, nor was the relationship of the French abbots at the German court anything but platonic.

THE ROMAN CANONICAL COLLECTIONS OF THE PERIOD OF GREGORY VII

PAUL FOURNIER

Paul Fournier (1853–1935), professor of Roman law and legal history at Grenoble, and later professor of the history of canon law at Paris, is known in this country only to a relatively small group interested in legal history. Trained as a paleographer at the École Nationale des Chartes and in Roman law, Fournier studied for thirty-five years the manuscripts containing collections of canon law between 850 and 1140 — roughly from the appearance of the *False Decretals* of Pseudo-Isidore to the *Decretum* of Gratian. His work was summed up in the two-volume study (published with the aid of his successor, Professor Gabriel LeBras), *History of the Canonical Collections in the West from the False Decretals to Gratian* (Paris, 1931–1932).

The present selection is the preamble of a long *Memoir*, presented to the Académie des Inscriptions et Belles-Lettres, which analyzes in detail the new collections of canon law inspired by Gregory VII. It shows how the reformers compiled new law books to give the reforming actions of the papacy the necessary solid legal basis to attain their ideals. Only from a sound canonical base could the Roman church assert and maintain its universal control.

THE reforms achieved or attempted in the Church were often presented as restorations of the discipline of the early centuries, which the new generations never ceased to consider the golden age of Christianity. And so it was also with the reform to which is attached the name of Gregory VII. That this manner of envisaging the great work of the Pontiff conformed to the reality of the facts, is a matter the historians do not fail to dispute. Without doubt, the evidence of antiquity furnishes the strongest possible arguments in favor of the fundamental principles of the reform: the obligation of celibacy for the clergy engaged in the higher orders and the condemnation of simony. But, when it concerns the application of these principles, the differences are considerable between the prescriptions of ancient times and those which Gregory VII and his fellow warriors claimed to make triumphant. Furthermore, the controversy a propos the the investitures, which assumed at this time grand importance, necessarily should not be confused with the questions raised by the condemnation of simony: this was truly a new problem stemming from circumstances which ancient Christianity did not know.

Be that as it may, it is enough to open the register of the letters of Gregory VII to be convinced that in any case this Pontiff was aided by the prescriptions and maxims of ancient law which he claimed to restore and designated by various names: *Decrees of the Holy Fathers, statutes, rule, doctrine, saying, authority, constitutions,*

Reprinted from "The Roman Canonical Collections of the Period of Gregory VII" by Paul Fournier in *Memoires* de L'Académie des Inscriptions et Belles-Lettres, Vol. XLI (Paris, 1918). [Translated by the editor of this volume.]

19

sanctions. Under these designations of a rather vague character, the Pope seemed to place at times decisions taken from the letters of his predecessors, and sparse rules from the works of ecclesiastical writers, known under the name of "Fathers," a list of whom was given in the famous decretal letter attributed to Pope Gelasius I; doubtless, one ought also to comprehend the canons of ancient councils recognized by the Roman church, which Gregory mentioned sometimes by the name of *sacred canons,* or *canonical traditions.* Such is the totality of rules to which the Supreme Pontiff referred ceaselessly; he was covered by their authority to make acceptable his decisions and defended himself willingly against the imputation, which his enemies did not fail to bring up, of innovating in contempt of past tradition. He liked to remark that he did not enunciate any new rule, *nihil novi, nihil adinventione nostra statuentes,* that in any manner he did not abandon the way his predecessors had traced for him. For example, when it concerned the election of bishops, he understood that it was done *secundum communem sanctorum Patrum intelligentiam et approbationem.* If it were a question of discarding some prelates who had wormed their way into ecclesiastical dignities under cover of illicit influence, he recalled that they were in opposition with "the pure and authentic authority of the Holy Fathers." It is to their teaching and their precepts that he sent back, never tiring, the clergy and the faithful of his time; it is in the precedents and the examples of ecclesiastical history that he liked to search for arguments.

However, seeing that the "Decrees of the Fathers" are the law of the clergy and the faithful, it is important to know where to find the text of this law. It is necessary in every society; but it was never more necessary than in the ecclesiastical society at the time of Gregory VII. To be convinced of it, it suffices to observe that the polemic which was born in the Western church, the great work of the reform, was above all patently marked by a juridical character; it is easy to get a clear idea of this by glancing at the numerous writings of this period where are found the arguments of the two parties. This is no reason to be astonished. In order to work the reform, the Pope set or renewed prohibitions destined to uproot the abuses. By force of circumstances, those who wished not to submit contested the legitimacy of these prohibitions or more or less discussed the bearing on the matter at hand. Whether they took one position or the other, they could not fail to raise questions of law. To resolve these questions they had to study the constitution of the Church and to scrutinize in principle and in development the plenitude of power of the Apostolic See. To arrive at the solution of other questions, it was indispensable to plunge into the exegesis of texts and to correlate them with earlier decisions. In any case they had to bring to light the foundations of the right to command that belonged to ecclesiastical authority and to interpret its commandments. Therefore it is to canonical prescriptions that the partisans and opponents of Gregory VII were forced incessantly to make their appeal.

No doubt at the middle of the XIth century, libraries of churches and monasteries did not lack collections containing canonical texts. There were to be found notably numerous manuscripts of the collection of the *Dionyso-Hadriana* and, in lesser number, manuscripts of the collection of Pseudo-Isidore. But those collections were composed in a chronological order; however, it was less the *chronological* collections than the *systematic* ones which lent themselves easily to daily use. Of these collections, the one most widely used and which could be called the manual of the canonist of the first half of the XIth century, was none other than the *Decretum,* composed about 1012 by the bishop of Worms, Burchard. About the same time there appeared in Italy a collection composed in five books, made up of ancient canons, numerous fragments taken from the Irish collection and various penitential books and, finally, texts of very different origins; the vogue of quite a number of works which proceeded from this collection was purely local and never left the Italian peninsula. It appears, however, that of those who knew the *Decretum* of Burchard, the Italian canonists were moved to combine the texts they took from this collection with those they likewise borrowed from the Collection in Five Books. Nevertheless, neither the *Decretum* of Burchard, nor the Italian collections met the requirements of Gregory VII and his partisans.

In fact, not only these collections, which begin with that of Burchard, contained texts of a doubtful origin and hence without authority, but also one found in abundance vague and idle dispositions, or resuscitating uselessly abrogated parts of Mosaic legislation; one struck here also some decisions in contradiction with the fundamental principles of Christian morality, as, for example, those from penitentials of Insular origin or even from the *Decretum* of Burchard which struck a blow at the indissolubility of marriage. In this way the canonical collections of the West had been invaded by texts which the Roman Church could not accept without close scrutiny: texts borrowed from Celtic or Anglo-Saxon Christianity, and also canons of the councils of the Frankish Church which, in many circumstances, had undergone more than it should influence of the barbarism of the invaders coming from across the Rhine. Furthermore and too often there were introduced into these collections some apocryphal materials, born of the fancy of their authors, of which one might say what the Council of Chalon of 813 said of penitential books of its time, "known errors of unknown authors." These criticisms are summarized in very vivid terms in the preface that the canonist, a contemporary and partisan of Gregory VII, the Cardinal Atto, placed at the top of his work, the *Capitulary,* which shall be treated further on. He complained of the multiplicity of apocryphal canonical texts, at the head of which he ranked the famous penitential called, "Roman," since at Rome one knew nothing about the author and Roman authority had never approved it. Really, he deplored the confusion into which ecclesiastical legislation had fallen — to such a depth that the members of the clergy no longer knew "what to hope, what to hold."

That confusion was due, Atto saw very clearly, to those earlier canonists who had fallen under the influence of varied currents that troubled the peaceful course of the stream issuing from Christian antiquity; they had taken texts from everywhere instead of accepting only those which were in the straight line of the Roman tradition. Also, for Atto and his fellow battlers the remedy appeared in a return to that tradition. To discard doubtful or exotic texts, and even canons of transalpine councils, that is to say, from the Frankish kingdom — so numerous in the *Decretum* of Burchard of Worms — which were occasionally at variance with the observance, or at least with the spirit of the Roman Church, to consider as illegitimate all the canons of councils to which the Holy See had not given its approbation expressed or tacit, these are the principal lines of the program of Atto. His colleague, Cardinal Deusdedit echoed him. He, also, in the prologue of the collection to which I shall soon call the attention of the reader, declared to admit the canons of the councils approved by the Roman Pontiff; it is true that he included in this category all the canons of the conciliar assemblies legitimately held before the Council of Chalcedon because, he said, the first canon of that Council had approved them *en bloc;* he put there also with Anastasius Bibliotecarius, not only the canons called *of the Apostles* that the Popes had sanctioned, but also the totality of rules and synodal constitutions conforming to the faith and Christian morality, which were not in contradiction with any decision of the Holy See. As wide as this interpretation might be, the principle of

Deusdedit is the same as that of Atto; it is further the principle of Gregory VII himself. To rely on texts proceeding from the Holy See or approved by it expressly or tacitly, is for the men of the school of Atto and Deusdedit, so to speak, for the entourage of Gregory VII, the sole means to reestablish the homogeneity and order in the legislation of the Church; it seemed that the anterior collection had appeared insufficient to them.

These men found also another flaw in the old collections. Doubtlessly at the beginning of their work they had used the good will of popular parties. But the passions of the masses are a dangerous instrument, apt to destroy as much as to edify; moreover, if the crowds had followed the reformers in Italy, it was not proven that they could be so docile in all parts of Christendom. It would have been easier for the partisans of Gregory VII to achieve their work if they had been able to obtain the aid of emperors, kings and dominant aristocrats; but the powerful of the earth drew too much advantage from the exploitation of dignities and ecclesiastical properties to second the efforts of those who wished to put an end to this exploitation and appeared thus like revolutionaries to these egoistic conservatives. The head of the Gregorian movement thus in being reduced to count principally on the internal strength of the spiritual power concentrated in the hands of the Roman pontiff; it is by the Pope and uniquely by the Pope that they had a chance to bring to its conclusion the work which they had undertaken. It is on this point, again, that the old collections were not in harmony with their aspirations.

In fact, that which mattered to them most, is to present in the frontispiece of the collections of which they should make use, the titles of the authority of the Apostolic See, and, by that, to bring together in a powerful bundle all the witness of the past, texts authentic or universally held as such, which lay in favor of the primacy of the Supreme Pontiff. Since the Papacy is the lever by which the Christian world ought to be uplifted, it is necessary to establish solidly this lever before putting it into action. Now, if the reformers had in their hands the collection of Pseudo-Isidore, rich in texts on which they could draw, this collection was not at all constructed in a systematic manner, so that the research in it was long and fatiguing. As for the systematic collections known to the middle of the XIth century, they were, from the point of view of the reformers, absolutely inadequate. In that of Burchard of Worms, very widely distributed, there had been inserted some of the texts essential for the founding of the rights of the Roman Pontiff, but without the author having taken care to put them in relief and having insisted upon multiplying the citations. The Italian collections of the first half of the XIth century are not less reserved, and one can say about the same of the only French canonical collection of this period, that of Abbo, abbot of Fleury-sur-Loire. Without doubt a canonist contemporary of Gregory VII had encountered in these several collections the elements of treatises bearing on the principal matters of ecclesiastical legislation, but he had not found in abundance the materials for a complete treatise on the Church and the authority of the Roman Pontiff. A single collection from the past might have been able to offer him a goodly number, the *Anselmo dedicata,* composed in Lombardy in the second half of the IXth century, but it had fallen into oblivion, especially in Italy.

For these different reasons the reformers had an imperious need of new collections. One should not be surprised that Gregory VII should have had a lively feeling for this need. A long time before he mounted the seat of St. Peter, at the time of the pontificate of Leo IX, he had addressed himself to St. Peter Damiani to ask him to collect in a small volume — *in parvi voluminis unionem* — the canonical fragments relative to the authority of the Holy See; he thought, further, he should join to it texts taken from the ecclesiastical historians which interpreted them and permitted to determine their bearing. Thus, from this time, Hildebrand for the defense of his work, appealed to ecclesiastical legislation as well as to history, and thus made a prelude to this renewal of canon law and to historiography which should mark his pontificate. In spite of the urging of Hildebrand, St. Peter Damiani did not defer to his wish. Later he regretted it; we know it by a letter which he wrote to Hildebrand following a mission with which he had been charged, in 1059, to reestablish the profoundly troubled order in the church of Milan. This mission gave St. Peter Damiani the occasion to appreciate the services that could be rendered by the collection which he had neglected to compose.

Other canonists were more docile to the exhortations of Gregory VII. There have been conserved four collections which were composed during his lifetime and at his inspiration. The oldest is the collection called *in 74 titles;* one shall see that this collection, quite short, was not long in becoming inadequate. When Hildebrand became Gregory VII, he provoked the composition of new collections. Three collections, still with us, date from his pontificate: that of Atto, titular cardinal of Saint Mark, that of Anselm, bishop of Lucca and one of the most devoted assistants of the Pontiff, in which he had every confidence, and, finally, that of Deusdedit, who was at that time cardinal-priest of the church of St. Peter-in-Chains. The collection of Anselm was composed as we know, at the order of Gregory VII. The cardinals Atto and Deusdedit, when, each in his turn, undertook an analogous work, had good reasons to think that in so doing they were responding to the wishes of the Pope. In truth, the work of Deusdedit was not completed until some months after the death of Gregory VII; but it reflected his thoughts and was composed completely during his reign. Thus, to appreciate the evolution of canon law at Rome under the personal action of Gregory VII, we should address ourselves to this collection as well as the other three mentioned. The object of this work is to study briefly each collection. If I am not mistaken, this study shall lead us to establish, in these various collections, the common traits which are manifest especially by the elimination of many texts of which the old authors had made use, and the employment of an important mass of materials which was unknown to them. The result is that the new collections, pushed to sources which were considered as strictly dependant on the tradition of the Mother Church are marked by a purely Roman character which distinguishes them sharply from all of the collections; they were destined by their authors to present canonical legislation purified and renewed by contact with antiquity.

LAY INVESTITURE AND ITS RELATION TO THE CONFLICT OF EMPIRE AND PAPACY

ZACHARY N. BROOKE

The selection from Professor Brooke's Raleigh Lecture, delivered before the British Academy, shows very clearly the careful, methodical analysis that is the hallmark of all his publications. A member of a family of academicians and scholars, Brooke graduated from Cambridge University. Except for the four years when he served in the Royal Artillery, his entire life was spent at Cambridge as a Fellow and later professor of mediaeval history. From 1921 he was a joint editor of the *Cambridge Medieval History* and in 1930–1931 served as Birkbeck Lecturer. His *English Church and the Papacy* was the first thoroughgoing study of the manuscripts of the early canon law as it applied to the Anglo-Norman Church. For the years of his retirement he had planned a large study of the Gregorian period but his failing health left the program unachieved. The student should note particularly Brooke's argument for the relative unimportance of the issue of lay investiture and mark well the difference between Brooke's and Barraclough's interpretation of the Lombard situation in this period.

AMONG the many issues at stake between the ecclesiastical and the secular authorities in the Middle Ages, there is none that has been given so dramatic a history as that of Lay Investiture during the brief period of its existence; its whole story is confined within the space of fifty years, from the first papal prohibition of it in 1075 to the settlement at Worms in 1122. There was a short prologue before 1075: papal decrees in 1059 and 1063, without indeed mentioning the word "investiture," had prepared the way for Gregory VII's decree; and an unofficial attack on it had been opened, probably in 1058, by Cardinal Humbert in his *liber adversus simoniacos*, followed a few years later by Peter Damian. There was no epilogue after 1122. The canonists registered the decrees, and Gratian in his *Decretum* published Gregory VII's canons of 1078 and 1080 and also canons of Paschal II, but by this time it was no longer a live issue. The lay power had surrendered the right to invest with ring and staff, and made no effort to revive the practice. Its sudden emergence, its sudden disappearance, alike distinguish it from other topics of controversy between the *regnum* and the *sacerdotium*. But in that controversy it has been given a peculiar, though as I consider a spurious, significance: during the half-century of its existence Empire and Papacy were engaged in almost continuous conflict, and this half-century is known in history as the period of the Investiture Struggle, the War of the Investitures.

Now, so far as the first part of that period is concerned, that is to say down to the death of Henry IV in 1106, it should be obvious that the struggle is not about investitures at all. The utterances of the two protagonists, the pamphlet literature of their supporters, make clear what was

Reprinted by permission from *Lay Investiture and Its Relation to the Conflict of Empire and Papacy* by Z. N. Brooke (Proceedings of the British Academy, Vol. XXV, 1939).

at stake. It was a struggle for supremacy between the *regnum* and the *sacerdotium*, between the heads of the secular and ecclesiastical departments, each side claiming that its power derives from God and that it has the right to judge and depose the other, while itself subject to no human judgement but to God alone. The settlement of this issue would automatically carry with it the settlement of all minor issues, such as lay investiture, which, in all their attacks upon one another and justifications of their own conduct, neither Henry nor Gregory troubled to mention, save for a brief reference to it in Gregory's letter to Henry in December 1075. However, a contest fought out over a supreme issue such as ultimate sovereignty will usually be provoked by a concrete case in which that sovereignty is concerned. Was Gregory VII's decree against lay investiture, as has so often been stated, the concrete case which led to the breach between him and the king? This view is undoubtedly a plausible one. The decree was issued in Lent 1075 and it was followed, in less than a year, by open warfare between the two powers. The conflict was practically continuous, for though interrupted by Henry IV's death in 1106 it was resumed almost immediately. The final settlement in 1122 was over the question of investiture; if this was the issue which was settled by the terms of peace, surely this was the issue about which the two powers had come to war.

Plausible as this reasoning is, it is unsound. The crisis in the relations between king and Pope occurred after, but not immediately after, the investiture decree; some nine months intervened, and during six of these at least relations between Gregory and Henry remained quite cordial. The breach happened after the decree, not because of it. Secondly, the interruption at 1106 was of short duration, but of the first importance. It was not a continuous struggle from 1076 to 1122; one contest ended in 1106 and another, a different one, began. The settlement in 1122 was a settlement of the issues raised in 1106, not of the much more important issue that was at stake in 1076. Contemporaries of the second struggle, looking back rightly to Gregory's decree as the source of their quarrel, might regard the contest as a continuous one from that point; contemporaries of the first struggle had no reason to make this mistake, and none of them attributes the cause of their conflict to the investiture decree. The cause was Henry's challenge to papal independence, or, from the other point of view, Gregory's challenge to royal independence. The concrete instance which occasioned the challenge of Henry, and provoked the Pope's counter-challenge, arose out of the situation at Milan; it was the question of the appointment and control of the archbishop of Milan that really provided the *casus belli*.

. . . Henry IV, when he became his own master in 1067, set himself the task of recovering the ground that had been lost since his father's death, and of all the usurpers of royal rights the Papacy was in his eyes the chief. How clearly does he show his purpose to follow in his father's footsteps when his brief moment of victory is vouchsafed to him; when in 1084 he was able to enter Rome to be crowned Emperor by Pope Clement, his nominee, after he had caused Pope Gregory to be deposed by a synod, thus repeating exactly what his father had done in 1046. But in his earlier days he had to walk warily; his power depended on Germany, and until it was assured there he was careful to keep on good terms with the Pope, even at the expense of some humiliation to the royal dignity. He was remarkably successful in Germany in those early years, and when he crushed a dangerous Saxon revolt it seemed that he had achieved the first part of his programme, and in 1071 could look to Italy, where indeed the situation demanded his close attention.

. . . It was not until the summer of 1075, some months after the investiture decree had been passed, that Henry regained the upper hand in Germany and was able once more to turn his attention to Italy. And once more Milan gave him the opportunity. The leader of the commune, Erlembald, was killed in a riot. The nobles and clergy temporarily recovered their former position and proceeded to elect a new archbishop of Milan, Tedald, whom Henry, regardless of his solemn pledge to the Pope, recognized as archbishop and conferred investiture on him by deputy. The commission sent by him for this purpose to Milan had instructions also to appoint and invest bishops to Fermo and Spoleto, which lay within the papal province, and to seek alliance with the Norman duke, Robert Guiscard; the king's plan was to surround and isolate the Papacy.

So, both in 1071 and in 1075, when the king felt himself in a position to intervene in Italy, the opportunity was provided by the situation at Milan. On the first occasion he was forced to withdraw owing to his disastrous set-back in Germany. In 1075 there was no withdrawal; Gregory took up the challenge to papal independence, and, after bitterly reproaching the king for his breach of faith, counter-attacked with the claim of papal authority over lay rulers, and the great issue was joined. In 1077 Henry made his peace with the Pope at Canossa (when no mention was made of investiture by either side), but after an uneasy truce of three years, the struggle broke out again in 1080, this time on Gregory's initiative, and only ended with Henry's death in 1106. What Henry felt about the investiture decree is impossible to say, as he never mentioned it; it is fair, however, to infer that it was an additional irritant to his mind. But by itself it had no influence on the course of events leading to the breach; they had no direct relation with it, and would have taken place if no decree against lay investiture had been issued. They began in 1071, four years before the investiture decree, and the issue was not whether the king could invest the archbishop of Milan, but whether king or Pope was to decide who

was to be archbishop. If Henry had been content to accept the papal candidate, Atto, in 1072, there is no reason to suppose that Pope Alexander II would have objected to Atto receiving investiture from the king; Gregory VII himself in 1073 ordered the new bishop of Lucca, Anselm, to avoid royal investiture only so long as the king remained out of communion with the Pope. In 1075 the papal indignation was expressed not at Henry's investing his new nominee, Tedald, but at his trying to set up a new archbishop in place of Atto, whom he had promised to recognize in 1073. So in this case, where the king himself had chosen his ground of attack, it was the control of appointments that was at stake. This was the immediate question which led to war, the preservation or the abolition of the lay control over the Church.

Lay control had centuries of tradition behind it. The lesser churches were subject to lay patronage, which practically meant lay ownership, the higher offices were usually at the disposal of kings or, in some cases in France, of powerful nobles. From the ecclesiastical point of view, the independence of the Church was at stake, and the newly reformed Papacy had come to recognize that lay control was the chief obstacle to the accomplishment of its programme. But control of the episcopate had become more than a tradition; to the rulers, particularly of Germany, it was both a political and an economic necessity. To maintain this control which was so necessary to them, the kings kept a close hand on elections and took care to see that the persons elected were attached primarily to their service. By the law of the Church, vague and ill-defined as yet, the election of a bishop rested with the clergy and people, as in the early days when the congregation in each town chose its own bishop. The election itself was supposed to be a matter for the clergy, among whom the cathedral clergy were coming to play the principal part, while the laity, often represented by the knights holding episcopal fiefs, were supposed to give their assent and support to the choice of the clergy. What actually happened when a vacancy occurred was that the electors had to obtain the king's leave to elect, and were often told by him whom they were to elect. If they tried to choose a candidate of their own, the king might refuse to ratify the election, and could make his will effective by withholding from such a candidate the temporalities, which during vacancy were in royal hands. First of all, then, the king could ensure an appointment satisfactory to himself, and this without infringing the canon law; for it would appear that the electors usually went through the formality of electing the king's nominee, so that the process approximated closely to the modern *congé d'élire*. Secondly, the king ensured the personal attachment and future services of the bishop-elect in the ceremony in which investiture took place. The king invested the bishop by handing to him the episcopal ring and the episcopal staff, which had been specially brought from the cathedral church of the bishopric, with the words *Accipe ecclesiam,* "Receive the church"; the bishop knelt before the king, did homage, and took an oath of fealty. Finally the bishop-elect was consecrated by the archbishop and bishops of the province. The king's control was thus assured, while the rule of canonical election was in most cases outwardly observed. One rule of the Church, however, was consistently ignored — that a candidate for office, whether priest or bishop, should be examined by his ecclesiastical superior and be rejected if unfit. It was the king and not the archbishop who satisfied himself as to the candidate's fitness for office.

. . . The abolition of the ceremony of royal investiture, while it would get rid of the manifest appearance of the king conferring ecclesiastical office and functions, would not really touch the heart of the question, for the royal authority over bishops and their appointments would remain unimpaired. But it was the first and most obvious point of attack. It was necessary

to start by making clear that spiritual functions, the priestly or the episcopal office, were not, and could not be, given by and received from a layman. In 1059, at Nicholas II's Council at the Lateran, a decree was passed that no cleric or priest was to obtain a church from a layman whether gratis or for money, and this was repeated at a council held in Rome by Alexander II in 1063. This lays down clearly the principle that the church — the spiritual office or function — is not to be given by a layman. Otherwise it is somewhat ambiguous in wording, as it is not clear whether it refers to the lower clergy only, and also whether, as the words seem to imply, it excludes lay patronage altogether. A canon of synods held at Vienne and Tours in 1060 is more precise: "no one henceforth is to receive a church, great or small, from a layman, without the consent of the bishop." The last words seem to indicate that the lesser clergy only are concerned, and that lay patronage is not excluded but confined to its lawful function of presentation.

In these decrees the ceremony of investiture is not directly attacked, but rather what was implied in it, and it would seem that at first attention was being directed to the lower churches. It was Gregory VII who in February 1075 officially mentioned investiture for the first time, and definitely applied the prohibition to the higher churches as well. So much can be said for certain, though we have not the wording of his decree. The canonists have no record of it, though Gratian includes both of Gregory's later decrees. And this is not due to chance. Certainly we might hope for information from the record of the Lenten synod of 1075 given in the Register of Gregory VII's letters; unfortunately that is very brief and is confined to an account of disciplinary measures. But the Pope himself does send to various archbishops and bishops decrees published by the synod; yet he makes no mention of the decree against lay investiture. He alludes to it rather vaguely in his letter to Henry

IV in December 1075. Not until 1077 does he make a direct mention of it, and then for the first time he orders its publication — by his legate, Bishop Hugh of Die, in France; and apparently it was published nowhere else. The decree was not, indeed, kept secret, but clearly the Pope took no immediate steps for its execution; later he could accept the excuses of two bishops (of Cambrai and Spires) that they had never heard of it. It seems strange that a decree so little known, and the enforcement of which was delayed until 1077, should have been regarded as responsible for the outbreak of the struggle between king and Pope at the end of 1075.

It may seem stranger still that a Pope so zealous and so strenuous in enforcing reform should have delayed so long the effective execution of this decree. Yet there is no real inconsistency in his behaviour. The investiture decree was not an end in itself, but a means to an end. The important thing for the right order and government of the Church was the appointment as bishops of men morally suitable and devoted to ecclesiastical and not to lay interests. If such were appointed, the manner of their appointment was of secondary importance; where the king was conscientious, as Henry III had been and as William the Conqueror was, the Pope raised no objection to royal influence. "It is the custom of the Roman Church," Gregory wrote in March 1078, "to tolerate some things, to turn a blind eye to some, following the spirit of discretion rather than the rigid letter of the law." But William was now the only ruler in whom he had confidence, so that elsewhere the manner of appointments became highly important. Even so, it was not a matter that could be dealt with brusquely. Gregory with his long experience of affairs had a keen sense of what was practical. Lay rulers did not placidly accept papal decrees which interfered with their traditional rights; thus the Papal Election Decree of 1059 had been bitterly resented at the imperial court, and Henry IV had not for-

gotten or forgiven it. The matter of investiture had to be handled tactfully, and if possible the king's consent obtained before it was openly enforced. From his letter to Henry IV in December 1075 we know that he sent the decree to the king and asked for his comments; he was ready to negotiate and if necessary to compromise. The situation was different in 1077, after Canossa; even then, it is in France that the decree is first issued, where royal opposition could easily be overborne.

Now, though the exact wording of the decree is nowhere recorded, it is possible to be clear as to its purport. . . . If we again call to our minds the ceremony, we can see exactly what it was that he prohibited — the king investing with ring and staff and using the words "Receive the church." "Our decree," says Gregory, "about the prohibition of investiture of this kind and the receiving of churches." The king was making "the gift of the bishopric," the spiritual office, and this must cease. The scope and importance of the investiture decree has been much exaggerated, because so much more has been read into it than it actually contains. Thus Professor Fliche and others have urged that, since the Pope did not expressly exclude the *temporalia* from the scope of his decree, it forbade investiture with temporalities as well as with spiritualities. Surely the contrary is much more probable. If Gregory had meant to include the temporalities in his prohibition he would have mentioned them, as Paschal II did in 1102; and as we shall see, when Gregory states his positive policy later on, in 1077, 1078, and 1080, he continues to be silent about the temporalities, and his only reference to the secular duties of the bishop is to state that he does not wish to interfere with them. In the controversial literature of the period the question whether the king could confer the temporalities was much debated, and very varying views were held by papalist writers. I cannot attempt an analysis of this controversial literature, and it has already been done admirably by Dr. Scharnagl. I entirely agree with his judgement that, while Cardinal Humbert would deny to the king all rights over the *temporalia*, it was not until after Gregory VII's death that the papalist writers again adopted this point of view. Thus Manegold of Lautenbach, writing at the very end of Gregory's papacy, contends that investiture with ring and staff is forbidden to the laity under all circumstances, but stigmatizes the statement of the royal supporters that Gregory was removing ecclesiastical benefices from all secular jurisdiction as a manifest lie; for in his decrees there is no mention of benefices at all, and as far as *temporalia* were concerned, it was only the possession of tithes by the laity that was prohibited. This is sound reasoning. We can understand that the royal supporters, having argued that royal investiture was concerned with temporalities only, would naturally declare that the decree prohibited the king from investing with the temporalities. The Pope, however, had prohibited investiture with ring and staff because it was clearly investiture with the spiritual functions. When he denounced the royal use of the words "Accipe ecclesiam," because *ecclesia* denoted spiritual office, his own prohibition of "investiture of this kind and the receiving of churches" must be taken to refer to the *spiritualia* alone, unless he expressly mentions the *temporalia*.

The investiture decree, therefore, while prohibiting the ceremony of investiture with ring and staff and the accompanying words, says nothing about the temporalities or the homage done by the bishop for them or his oath of fealty. Its purpose was to remove all suggestion that the ecclesiastical office, the spiritual functions, could be conferred by a layman. It was, as has been said, a means towards an end, and the end was the appointment of the right men as bishops. It was only a step in that direction, for Gregory knew that, even if the ceremony of lay investiture was abandoned, secular considerations would still prevail in the creation of a bishop. His mind was set on good appointments, and

this meant the upsetting of the first part of the customary procedure. Both of these points are emphasized in a letter he wrote to the clergy and people of Aquileia in September 1077, a letter which shows signs of having been written at the Pope's personal dictation. "That which in the Church has long been neglected owing to sin and corrupted by evil custom, we desire to renew and restore to the honour of God and the salvation of all Christendom, namely that to rule the people of God in every church, when the moment arises such a bishop shall be elected and in such a way that in accordance with the judgement of Truth he may not be termed a thief and a robber, but be worthy to bear the name and office of shepherd. This is indeed our will, this is our desire, this by the mercy of God will be, so long as we live, our unwearied aim." "But," he goes on to say, "that which pertains to the service and fealty due to the king, we do not wish to contradict or to prevent. And so we are trying to introduce nothing new, nothing of our own invention, but that alone do we seek, which the salvation and need of all men requires, that in the ordaining of bishops in accordance with the common understanding and approval of the holy fathers, first of all the evangelic and canonical authority should be preserved." Notice the words "nothing new, nothing of our own invention." These were the same words as he had used about his investiture decree in his letter to Henry IV in December 1075. It was not new to forbid kings to give ecclesiastical offices; it would have been new, he implies, for him to interfere with the services due to the king for the temporalities.

What he is anxious to do, then, is to preserve canonical authority in the appointment of bishops, and he makes clear in this letter that two points are of the first importance — canonical election and the examination of the candidate by his ecclesiastical superior. He tells the clergy and people of Aquileia that he is sending legates to see that their recent election of a patriarch was rightly conducted, and that they have chosen a person who by his life, character, and learning is fitted for the office. (As the election of a patriarch is in question, the Pope implies that he is the ecclesiastical superior who decides this.) Then, at the November synod of 1078 he issued a canon declaring to be null and void all appointments "in which payment of money, canvassing, or deference to an individual played a part, or which were not made by common consent of clergy and people in accordance with canonical regulations, and were not approved by those whose function it was to consecrate." At the Lenten synod of 1080 a canon, which immediately precedes the second and definitive excommunication of Henry IV, put in a positive form what had been put negatively in 1078. "Whensoever, on the death of the pastor of any church, another has to be appointed canonically in his place, on the instance of the bishop-visitor, who has been sent there by the apostolic see or by the metropolitan, the clergy and people, setting aside all secular ambition, fear, and favour, with the consent of the apostolic see or their own metropolitan are to elect to themselves a pastor under God. If corrupted by some vice they shall presume to act otherwise, they shall lose all fruit of their election wrongly made; they shall have no further power of electing, which shall rest upon the deliberation of the apostolic see or of their own metropolitan." Here then is Gregory's positive policy expressed, and it is expressed, at those very councils in which he issued the decrees against lay investiture which have come down to us. Those decrees forbade only one part of the ordinary procedure, the actual ceremony of investiture, and apart from decrees against simony and clerical marriage this was all that was done in 1075. But in 1078 and 1080 there is a great difference. Not only is the prohibition of the offensive ceremony repeated, but a great deal of the rest of the customary procedure is condemned — everything, in fact, which concerned the appointment of the bishop

except the reception by him of the *temporalia* and the service and fealty due therefrom to the king. Canonical election is to be a reality, not a formality; the initiative is to lie with Pope or metropolitan, not with the king; clergy and people are to unite in free choice, not to obey lay dictation; the person of the bishop-elect must be approved by the consecrator, not by the king; and if these conditions are not fulfilled, the election is void and the choice of a bishop devolves on Pope or metropolitan.

If this programme in its entirety had been carried into practice, it would have produced almost a revolution in political as well as in ecclesiastical conditions. It left to the king only the right of bestowing the temporalities and receiving due services in return; it denied to him any part in the appointment of those who were to receive the temporalities from him. The effect would be very serious for him, far more serious than that created by the abolition of lay investiture. In spite of this, Gregory no longer feels it necessary to act circumspectly, and to try by negotiation to obtain the king's consent. Doubtless these decrees have special reference to Germany and Italy; in France his legates have the upper hand and the enforcement of canonical regulations is within their power; when their authority extended to Normandy there was friction with William I, but Gregory was anxious to avoid a contest with a king whose appointments were at any rate in keeping with the spirit, if not the letter, of the ecclesiastical regulations. Hitherto he had not denied to the king of Germany some part in appointments, and as late as July 1075 he wrote asking for Henry's assistance in the appointment of a successor to bishop Hermann of Bamberg, who had been deposed for simony. But with the change in the political situation came a complete change in his attitude. He had sat in judgement on the king, and after Canossa, and particularly after the election at Forchheim of Rudolf as rival to Henry, he felt himself to be in a position to lay down the law. He claimed that the decision between the two kings must rest with him, and he continually announced that he would decide for the one with whom was righteousness. The sign of the righteous ruler was, in the teaching of St. Augustine and Gregory the Great, obedience to the commandments of God and therefore by inference to the Church which interprets God's will. So Gregory VII felt that he could now proclaim the complete canonical doctrine and expect obedience. Rudolf's supporters were careful to show how scrupulous their leader was in refraining from interfering with ecclesiastical appointments and from investing with ring and staff, limiting his part to the bestowal of the temporalities after consecration (notice that this is regarded as perfectly lawful), while Henry flagrantly violated the papal decrees. There is every reason to credit their account, for Henry felt himself entirely within his rights in maintaining the customary practice, while Rudolf was anxious to avoid giving any offence to the Pope, whose recognition and support he needed. Probably this was one of the chief considerations which caused Gregory to give his decision at last in 1080, when he declared Henry deposed for ever because of his pride, disobedience, and falsehood, and assigned the kingdom to Rudolf because of his humility, obedience, and truthfulness. The repetition at the same time of the investiture decree, accompanied by the positive statement of the law of the Church on canonical elections, seemed now to be a programme which could be straightforwardly achieved. As events showed, his optimism, both in 1078 and in 1080, was unjustified. As he could not execute his sentence against Henry, he could not carry out his ecclesiastical programme. There was not even a contest about this programme, which, while naturally accepted by the German rebels, was as naturally disregarded by Henry's adherents, who had a Pope of their own. The issue could not become a live one until Henry IV was dead and Empire and

Papacy were once more in communion.

The prohibition of lay investiture, as we have seen, by itself made no difference to the effective control of the episcopate by the king. When it was linked up by Gregory VII in 1078 and again in 1080 with decrees which reversed the traditional method of appointment, it became part, though not the most important part, of a programme which set in sharp opposition the vital interests of *regnum* and *sacerdotium*. After Gregory's death there is a marked change. In place of his emphasis on the illegality of the customary method of appointment, it is the subordination of bishops to the king in respect of their temporalities that is attacked. The view of Cardinal Humbert, that investiture with the *temporalia* as well as with the *spiritualia* should be denied to laymen, begins to reappear, not at first in official decrees but in the writings of papal partisans. However, the Pope himself soon opens an attack upon the feudal subordination of bishop to king, which had been an accompanying feature of the ceremony of investiture, but on which Gregory VII himself had made no pronouncement. Victor III at Benevento in 1087, Urban II at Melfi in 1089 and again at Piacenza in 1095, had been content to repeat Gregory VII's decree forbidding any ecclesiastic to receive investiture of any ecclesiastical office from a layman. It was at the Council of Clermont in 1095, where he preached the First Crusade, that Urban II first gave official expression to the new policy. After canons prohibiting any ecclesiastic from receiving a church or any lay office from the hand of a layman, and kings or princes from giving investiture of any ecclesiastical office, there followed a canon "that no bishop or priest was to do fealty as a vassal to a king or any layman." In 1099 at Rome, shortly before his death, he repeated these decrees. . . .

The day after they had heard the Pope pronounce these solemn words, Anselm and Eadmer started on their return journey to England, and on his arrival Anselm was at once engaged in a conflict with the new king, Henry I. From the beginning it was embittered by the fact that bishops were forbidden not only to receive investiture from the king but also to do homage. The new Pope, Paschal II, went farther than Urban II and alined himself with the extreme reformers, when in 1102, besides forbidding the clergy to receive churches from lay hands, he forbade them also to receive church property from laymen. Prohibition of lay investiture became a much more vital issue when these other prohibitions, which affected the *temporalia* as well as the *spiritualia,* were tacked on to it. Paschal's own addition was sent by him to Anselm in April 1102. So the investiture decree came first to England when Anselm brought it on his return from Rome; when it did come it was linked on to the other decree which forbade the homage of bishops to the king; and soon this further addition was linked on as well.

. . . But when Henry IV died in 1106, his son Henry V, who had previously been restored to communion, recognized Paschal II as the lawful Pope and could no longer ignore papal decrees so repeatedly published during the long period of schism. Henry V had allied with the Papacy to bring about the downfall of his father, but it had been the weakness of the royal power which had led him into rebellion, and his desire to prevent it from getting still weaker before he succeeded to the throne. The diminution of royal rights was, therefore, the one thing he would not countenance. So, though Henry IV's death brought the great issue between Empire and Papacy to an end, it left other unsolved issues which immediately embittered the relations between the two powers. Henry V refused to accept the decrees against lay investiture, and a contest began which was truly an Investiture Contest. The controversial literature flared up again, but this time it is solely devoted to the question of investiture. The king's supporters usually declared that the king was only investing with the *temporalia;* his opponents refuted

them with arguments similar to those used by Cardinal Humbert and Peter Damian, but they were not themselves in agreement as to whether investiture with the *temporalia* was in itself unlawful. Henry V having opposed the first stage in the new papal programme, the prohibition of investiture with ring and staff, the controversy ranged mainly about that point; and the additional canons, though they considerably aggravated the issue, received comparatively little attention. . . .

The eventual settlements, with the king of England in 1107 and with the Emperor in 1122, were very similar: in effect, both kings agreed to renounce their practice of investing with ring and staff provided that the other canons were not pressed. In England, Paschal II allowed Anselm to consecrate bishops who had done homage, provided the king abstained from investing; this, intended by him to be a temporary concession, was treated as a permanent one by Henry I, and the persistence of the customary procedure is shown in the Constitutions of Clarendon. Calixtus II's concession to Henry V at Worms was a carefully drawn legal document. In return for Henry's renunciation of investiture, it recognizes the king's share in the elections of German bishops and abbots, especially when the elections were contested; the regalia were to be received from the king by a touch of the sceptre; and the bishop or abbot was to do homage and take the oath of fealty to the king before consecration. The Pope, therefore, obtained the abolition of the objectionable ceremony of investiture with ring and staff, but all the rest of the customary procedure was maintained. Canonical elections took place, but clearly not free elections, since they were to be held in the king's presence; no mention is made of examination by the consecrator; and the additions introduced by Urban II and Paschal II to Gregory's decree against investiture have disappeared. Lay control over appointments and over the personnel of the episcopate remains unchanged. All that has happened is that what Gregory VII forbade in 1075 has been abolished. . . .

It is instructive here to notice how different was the course of events in France. There was considerable friction but no open conflict, and there was no formal concordat. The royal power was so weak in the eleventh century that Gregory VII was able to establish permanent legates — Hugh bishop of Die and Amatus bishop of Oloron — who held numerous councils, and, in spite of constant opposition from the king, were often able to enforce the execution of their decrees. We have seen that the decree against lay investiture was openly published first in France, and it seems to have had its principal effect there; certainly by the twelfth century the king has ceased to invest with ring and staff. At the same time the king ceased to nominate to bishoprics, so that election in accordance with canonical regulations was becoming the rule. He still exercised an influence on the election, especially when it was contested, and he retained his right of confirming elections, which was certainly no mere formality. In place of investiture he conceded the temporalities of the see, and the bishop took an oath of fealty, usually after his consecration, but did no homage. The king was thus left with a certain voice in elections, sometimes a decisive voice, though the initiative had passed from him to the electors; it was recognized that the temporalities were held from him, and services were due to him in return. Usually he could count on the loyalty of the bishops, even against the Pope. . . .

The year 1122 marks the end of a chapter. The dispute about lay investiture is over; the question is settled once and for all. It only remains to look back over these fifty years of tragic strife and summarize the conclusions of the survey I have been attempting to give. The main purpose of Gregory VII in the early years of his Papacy was that the Church should be properly governed, and therefore that the right men should be appointed to hold office and to have the cure of souls. But the offices were being filled with men whose qualification was their capacity for secular administration. The lay rulers controlled appointments in their own interests and not in that of the Church, and to gain office the clergy canvassed, curried favour, spent large sums of money; against this offence, simony, the reformers had already been fighting a long and apparently unsuccessful battle. Success, Gregory saw, could only be won if lay control, which resulted in bad appointments and encouraged the practice of simony, was abolished. He felt it to be obligatory on him to rescue the Church from the stranglehold of the lay power, so that it could be free to conduct its elections in accordance with its own regulations. He made his first aim not at the means by which that control was exercised and maintained, but at the ceremony which was the outward and visible sign of that control, in which the king invested with ring and staff and so gave the spiritual office. His decree in 1075 prohibited that part of the ceremony and nothing more. It was not an end in itself, but a first step towards the real end of proper appointments to ecclesiastical offices — a necessary step, to make clear that the hold of the laity over the spiritual functions, which this ceremony portrayed, was illegal. It was a grave matter, likely to lead to conflict, though Gregory, misled by the compliant attitude of the king, hoped that it would not and that some composition could be arranged by mutual consent; possibly if Henry received assurances about the *temporalia* he would be willing to abandon the *spiritualia*. However, against Gregory's purpose was set the purpose of Henry IV, determined to relax none of his control but rather to regain what had been lost during his unfortunate minority, when the Papacy which his father had dominated had become independent. As soon as success came to him in Germany, he grasped the opportunity afforded by the situation at Milan and challenged a conflict which involved the major issue between the *regnum* and *sacerdotium*; and while that conflict was raging there was no place for consideration of a subordinate issue such as lay investiture.

So comes the first intermission. Thereafter the Pope, with the impression of victory strong upon him, proceeded to his more positive aim. He abandons the idea of negotiation and begins to enforce his decree. Twice he reissues it, in 1078 and 1080, and couples with it decrees enjoining free canonical election and examination of the candidate by his ecclesiastical superior, which if they could be enforced would ensure that the purpose for which the investiture decree had been promulgated would be achieved. The schism, renewed in 1080, again made the fulfilment of his purpose impossible. With his death in 1085, there is a change of motif. For his successors, while they continually repeated his decree against lay investiture, did not use it for the purpose for which he had intended it. With him it had been the spiritual work of the bishop that mattered, so he had concentrated on the method of appointment; they concentrated on the temporal possessions and services, which he had ignored. They used the decree, not so much as a means to the end of good appointments, but rather as a means towards depriving the king of all control over the bishop when appointed. They added to it decrees forbidding homage to be done by clerics to laymen, and forbidding the clergy to receive their temporalities from lay hands. When the long schism came to an end, this was the situation with which the new king of Germany was faced. Investiture is now of prime importance, its removal an end in itself, since the other decrees are nugatory without it. Its abolition is therefore the one desideratum with the papal party. But by concentrating upon it they lost their ultimate aim. The king had something with which to barter; by renouncing investiture he gave up the shadow and retained the substance — all that part of the customary procedure which ensured his control over the appointment of bishops and over the bishops when appointed. So Gregory's purpose was defeated when what he intended as a means became an end. It was a Pyrrhic triumph for the Papacy when the king was left in possession of the field.

THE CLUNIACS IN ENGLAND

DAVID KNOWLES

Regius Professor of Modern History at the University of Cambridge since 1954, Dom David Knowles, O.S.B., has no peer today in the realm of monastic history. Born in 1896 and educated at Cambridge and Rome, Professor Knowles entered the Order of St. Benedict in 1914. Since 1946 he has taught at Cambridge and published four authoritative volumes on the history of the monastic and religious orders in England to their dissolution in the sixteenth century.

This selection from *The Monastic Order in England* offers a thoroughly up-to-date view of how the Cluniac movement was constituted and what is meant by *monastic* reform in the tenth and eleventh centuries. If the student will weigh the conclusions of Sackur along with the description of Professor Knowles, the question of the nature of Cluniac influence in the Gregorian period should begin to appear in a new light.

THE developments recorded in the preceding pages do not exhaust the list of new movements set on foot by the Normans, for no mention has as yet been made of the Cluniac foundations. The influence of the great monastic reform which took its rise and maintained its seat in the celebrated Burgundian abbey had already twice affected the course of English monastic history before Cluny herself had any dependencies in this country. The revival under Dunstan had received a deep impress from Fleury, which in its turn owed its renaissance wholly to Cluny; similarly, the Norman monasticism, with the partial exception of Bec and her daughters, could trace a large measure of its spirit and almost all its uses back through William of Dijon to Maieul and Odo of Cluny. But while it is true to say that almost all black monk houses south of Lorraine and the Rhine owed their new life, or a large part of it, to the stream that had its rise at Cluny — and recent scholarship has shown the Cluniac affinities of almost all French customals of the late tenth and early eleventh centuries — yet it is equally true to say that what these various centres received was not any specific variety of black monk life, but simply the life and observance typical of the epoch in its most active form. In other words, before the beginning of the eleventh century Cluny did not stand out clearly as the head of a new constitutional organization or as the representative of tendencies peculiar to herself, but simply as a monastery concerned to impart to others the great essentials of the liturgical monastic life as they were conceived and expressed by her. Nor did she, before the end of the tenth century, bind to herself by any external constitutional framework the abbeys which she had reformed.

Under Odilo, abbot from 994 to 1049, a change gradually came about. Partly because experience showed that monasteries at the death of a reforming abbot or of his immediate disciples fell back into disorganization or came under the control of secular rulers or proprietors, but more because the whole of society was becoming conscious of capabilities for closer organization, Cluny

Reprinted by permission from *The Monastic Order in England* by David Knowles, pp. 145–150 (Cambridge University Press, 1940).

now began to bind to herself in varying degrees of dependence the monasteries over which her abbot had been given reforming power or which desired to adopt Cluniac customs, and whereas in the tenth and early eleventh centuries the abbots of Cluny had been content to reform by imposing Cluniac uses and by temporary supervision, the tendency grew to deprive monasteries of their autonomy, and even to draw back into the system houses previously reformed, but left independent. What was first noticeable under Odilo developed under Hugh, often called the Great, and in his long reign (1049–1109), which may in many ways be taken to cover the apogee of Cluny's long course of splendour, and during which the chief English plantations were made, the constitution of the Cluniac system of government reached something of an equilibrium.

That system has often been described, though too often an account has been given of the state of fullest development in the later twelfth century without any notice of the gradual stages by which it was evolved. In its fullest extension, indeed, it was not wholly of domestic inspiration, but had adopted several important features, such as a general chapter and visitations, from the reform movements of the twelfth century. To describe it therefore *sans phrase* as a fully developed religious order and as the first of its kind in the Middle Ages, with the abbot of Cluny as General, is not strictly true of even the latest stage, and is historically misleading. In its eleventh-century form, when it was still a growth untouched from outside, it was in no sense an order, but rather a body of head and members loosely knit together by bonds resembling those of contemporary feudal institutions. Its constitution was not a scientific, logical, legal creation like that of the Cistercians and their imitators, but a hierarchy of relationships culminating in personal dependence upon the abbot of Cluny. There was no balance, no coordination in it, still less any anticipation of the elective and judicial elements of the later orders of friars. It is not even possible to say that it was a stage in the evolution of the "order," save that the existence of the vast Cluniac body showed at once the possibility and the dangers of the dependence of a large number of houses upon a single head.

In the second half of the eleventh century the widespread Cluniac organization was made up of four classes: Cluny herself, with her satellite cells depending immediately upon her; a few monasteries belonging to the system and sharing Cluniac uses and privileges but retaining abbots of their own; priories, which in importance and numbers were the equals of large abbeys but which received their superior at the hands of the abbot of Cluny; and, finally, lesser priories and cells depending as a rule upon their founding house in the same way that the latter depended upon Cluny. The monks of all these houses ranked as monks of Cluny and when at Cluny were considered children of the house; there was, however, a distinction between those of the second and those of the third and fourth classes. Novices of one of the abbeys were clothed and professed by their own abbot; novices of a dependent priory were received to the habit there with the permission of the abbot of Cluny, but could be professed only by the abbot of Cluny himself. In theory, therefore, the vows were taken to the abbot of Cluny and pronounced there in his presence, and even as late as Ulrich's day, *c.* 1070, the custom continued of novices coming up to Cluny on the feast of SS. Peter and Paul to make profession, though they were allowed three years' grace in which to do it. Distance clearly made this impossible of observance in all cases, and alternatively the novices could be professed or at least receive the blessing of their habit at the hands of the abbot of Cluny when on his rounds of the dependencies. But in such cases they still had to present themselves at Cluny to make or repeat their profession to the mother-house, thus vowing "stability" a second time — an anomaly which did not escape criticism at the hands of the early Cistercians. The unwieldiness of this system caused frequent and whole-sale transgressions, and Peter the Vener-able, in the first half of the twelfth century, records both the widespread, unauthorized reception of novices and a delay of ten or even thirty years in proceeding to Cluny for blessing or profession.

Over all houses the abbot of Cluny exer-cised in theory at least supreme, plenary and immediate power, and was therefore constantly occupied in journeys and visits, but the frequency and procedure of these visits were fixed by no kind of legislation, nor did any machinery exist by which the responsibility and labours of the abbot could be lessened by means of a delega-tion or devolution of powers. In practice, therefore, a very great measure of inde-pendence was left to local superiors, es-pecially those at a distance from Cluny, and in England, if nowhere else, founders often succeeded in inserting clauses en-suring a certain degree of freedom into the charter of gift. And, although vows were taken to the abbot of Cluny, the monks of dependent priories remained for all practical purposes under the jurisdiction of the local superior all their lives; there was no constant interchange of personnel as in the later centralized orders. Finally, the custom grew up of exacting from the houses founded or adopted by Cluny a yearly tribute, varying in amount and in itself of no great significance, but which in the aggregate brought in a considerable sum. This was the equivalent of the *census* paid to the Holy See by the churches through-out Europe which were in a special way under its protection.

Such in brief outline was the organiza-tion of the Cluniac body during the later years of St. Hugh — supreme and imme-diate (though often limited) control by the abbot of Cluny; appointment by him of the superiors of all houses immediately de-pending upon Cluny; profession of all to Cluny and (in theory at least) at Cluny; and the payment of a small annual tribute.

The whole body was bound together by a common acceptance of the customs and uses of Cluny and by the decrees of suc-cessive abbots.

Alongside of this constitutional develop-ment there was evolving at the same time a very definite spirit or programme within the mother-house, which inevitably spread in greater or less degree to her depend-encies. Considered from the point of view of observance, this took the form of an in-crease in the number of psalms and prayers recited daily, together with an ever-growing elaboration of ceremonial in the perform-ance of the liturgy; considered from the point of view of discipline, it consisted in extreme attention to regularity and uni-formity in the performance of all corporate duties. Together, the observance and dis-cipline of Cluny eliminated all extra-litur-gical activity for the monks following the life of the greater houses, and thus Cluny had little or no share in the educational and intellectual revivals of the period, and her monks produced little artistic work within the cloister. A climax was reached in the central period of the long reign of St. Hugh; alike in splendour of ceremonial, tireless activity in performance, and regu-larity of large masses of monks. Cluny in the third quarter of the eleventh century presented a spectacle without parallel in Europe, and the larger dependencies and those influenced most directly by her shared these characteristics in their meas-ure, and indeed continued to exhibit them when a decline had begun to set in at Cluny herself.

But at the time of the Conquest, despite the great size to which the body had al-ready attained the heart would seem still to have been possessed of remarkable soundness. In 1049 Cluny had received as abbot, in succession to the long-lived St. Odilo, the young priest Hugh, of the highest nobility in blood and, as it already seemed to all, of predestinate sanctity, who although only twenty-five at his election had already been for some years in supreme charge of the discipline of the house as grand prior. He was in the event to rule for sixty years, during which period both he and his abbey were invested with an aureole of veneration comparable to, though very different from, that surrounding Clairvaux and its abbot in the fifty years that followed Hugh's death. The impression of sanctity given by Hugh and his community, at least until c. 1080, is vouched for by such weighty testimony of contemporaries that it is unnecessary to take space to record it. The enthusiastic praises of Peter Damian, the veneration to which Gregory VII gave expression on more than one occasion in public and private, the reverence with which the Conqueror regarded Hugh, the impression produced by Cluny on William de Warenne and his wife — these are but a few typical instances out of the many that could be adduced. In assessing their force we must, however, remember that in the fifth decade of the century the current was only just beginning to set in the direction of reform at Rome, that the monasteries of Romuald and John Gualbert and Peter Damian made no display to the outer world, and that the new Norman religious life was as yet unknown to Europe at large. Everywhere, and especially in the most populous parts of Germany and north Italy, "nicolaism" and simony were rife, and the spectacle of Cluny, a little world in itself given wholly to the worship of God in a setting of incomparable splendour and untouched by secular intrigue, must have been dazzling enough to those who in Italy and elsewhere were striving in the dust and darkness for better things.

Moreover, the ideal for which Cluny stood, its message to the world, was one not hard to comprehend. It was the regular, tireless, all but ceaseless liturgical service carried out by the great numbers of a highly disciplined army, using every means of chant, of ceremony and of ornament available to render that service more solemn and more splendid. This tireless, disciplined service — the *districtio ordinis* of so many witnesses — was, and remained

for a century, the distinguishing note of Cluniac monasticism. To this, we have explicit testimony over the whole period. When, about 1059, the young Anselm, full of the desire for learning, was debating whither to turn in the religious life, he rejected the possibility of Cluny on account of the *districtio ordinis* prevailing there — that is, not the physical austerity or spiritual fervour of the life (for both of these were to be found at Bec also) but the rigorous observance which kept the monks occupied in choir and therefore rendered study impossible. Some four years later we have the witness of Peter Damian. Using the same phrase (*ordo districtus*) he observes that when he was at Cluny, at midsummer, 1063, the monastic duties, and particularly those of the choir, were so prolonged that even in the longest days of the year, when sleep according to the Rule would have been shortest, the monks could hardly find half an hour's free time in the day at their disposal. He praises such a system, remarking that with their time so occupied the monks could scarcely commit any sin save one of thought. Ulrich's *Consuetudines,* committed to writing some fifteen or twenty years later, enable us to verify Peter Damian's statement with precision. Speaking of the same days of midsummer, he tells us of the continuous sequence of offices which reduced the time for sitting and speaking in the cloister to a vanishing point; the whole framework and clocktime of the day, indeed, was artificially dislocated in the interests of the liturgy: Ulrich tells us that the night office on the feast of SS. Peter and Paul (29 June) began by daylight on the evening previous and lasted till daybreak; in order to obtain the requisite hours of sleep everything on the previous day after the High Mass was telescoped, and compline on the vigil was sung at the hour of suntime (c. 2:15 p.m.) at which on the following day the monks were singing none. On days of any solemnity, indeed, there was little if any cessation of conventual duty (in the main choral) between mattins, which often began before midnight, and the end of High Mass the following day about noon. With such a horarium in mind we shall not wonder at the anecdote told by the Cluny chronicler of Abbot Hugh and Peter Damian: that when the latter praised all at Cluny save the quantity and quality of food and drink, which exceeded that allowed by the Rule, he received the reply that before making such a criticism he should himself spend a week in following exactly the daily order of life, and that he would then confess that it could not be executed on such sparing fare.

This, then, was the life which, still lived with enthusiasm and still attracting those with the highest aspirations in central and southern France, passed under chosen leaders to Bermondsey and Lewes in England and which, when the twelfth century had passed its second decade, still evoked the admiration of William of Malmesbury and King Henry I.

THE GREGORIAN PROGRAMME

RALPH FRANCIS BENNETT

Ralph F. Bennett, presently lecturer and tutor at Magdalene College, Cambridge, has published various studies on the Middle Ages and is occupied with editing the works of William of Ockham. For the translation of G. Tellenbach's *Church, State and Christian Society at the Time of the Investiture Contest* (1940), Bennett wrote an *Introduction*, a part of which follows, which summarizes an important interpretation of the Gregorian epoch.

IT is no part of the purpose of this introduction to recapitulate what Professor Tellenbach has to say. It is sufficient to remark that he distinguishes three main attitudes on the part of the Church: (i) the ascetic, based on withdrawal from the world; (ii) the sacerdotal, based on conversion of the world by the priestly hierarchy; (iii) the monarchic, based on the conversion of the world by the action of a divinely-instituted kingship to which the clergy should be subordinate — here, of course, it comes into conflict with the sacerdotal outlook — and not by a clerical hierarchy subject to the bishop of Rome.

The attitude of withdrawal, which was dominant in the early centuries of Christianity, could be reconciled with the conception of monarchical control; devout men, withdrawing from a world which did not interest them because they regarded it as fundamentally evil, were content to leave secular society to be ordered by the kingship. The sacerdotal point of view, which exalted the power of the priest and regarded it as his duty to convert the world and lead it to the Kingdom of God, could not accept the monarchy in this way. There are, then, in reality only two lines of thought: withdrawal, which is reconcilable with the theocratic monarchy, and conversion, which is not, because it must involve the subjection of lay society to the priestly authority. The interaction of these two tendencies in Christianity, writes Professor Tellenbach, has at all times been of vital importance, and they ultimately determined the course of the reform movement in the tenth and eleventh centuries. The chief interest of the pontificate of Gregory VII is the fact that it marked the final rejection by the official Church of the old attitude of mistrust towards the world. To Gregory, this attitude had no meaning; his historic rôle was to enunciate logically and unequivocally the opposite principle, the conversion of the world by the priesthood.

This was the positive side of his task, and for its successful execution there was one indispensable prerequisite: that the world should be ready to accept the claim of Christianity to be the moral basis upon which its affairs should rest. This is an aspect of the age of Canossa which is sometimes too little stressed; both parties approached the quarrel from a high ethical standpoint, neither grounded its actions solely upon considerations of power-politics (this applies with particular force to the argument that, in view of the governmental system set up by Otto I, the emperors needed complete control of Church appointments within their territories lest

Reprinted by permission from the "Introduction" by Ralph F. Bennett to Gerd Tellenbach, *Church, State, and Christian Society at the Time of the Investiture Contest* (Oxford: Basil Blackwell, 1940).

the government itself should collapse — an argument which is sometimes accorded an importance greater than it deserves), both really felt that they were right in the fullest sense of the word and that their claims were in accordance with the will of God. Many things had contributed towards the attainment of this situation — the first victory of the principle of conversion in St. Augustine's *De Civitate Dei,* the theocracy of Charlemagne and the wide extent of the proprietary system, to mention only a few — and even something approaching a dissolution of society, caused by the invasions of Saracens, Norsemen and Magyars in the ninth and tenth centuries, had been unable to prevent its development: the popularity of the reforming movement with all classes of the laity amply demonstrates the truth of this statement. In one way, then, the interest of the Investiture Contest lies in the fact that it deserves to be set beside the missionary journeys of St. Paul and Constantine the Great's edict of Milan as one of the few notable steps in the long process by which the Christian religion has sought to lead the world to complete acceptance of its principles and to incline it towards the canons of conduct laid down in the Gospels. This is a process which Catholic and Protestant have equally at heart, and it is of particular interest at the present time, when it seems to many that the root cause of our ills is the very incompleteness of the process; there is a painful abundance of force in the contention that a new step forward is needed — a step forward by the whole of society, akin to that which not only made possible the work of Gregory VII but also set the tone for the arguments used on both sides throughout the earlier part of the Investiture Contest.

On the negative side, Gregory's task could only be the destruction of the hitherto dominant régime in Church and State; and this involved, as its primary object, the attempt to deprive princely dominion over the Church of the divine and sacramental character in which it had so long appeared.

The "right order in the world" could not be established until this object had been secured, since, in Gregory's eyes, the "right order" implied the existence of a "free" Church in a reorganised society. This part of his programme clearly amounted to an attack upon the political institutions of his time, and the question at once arises, "Was Gregory a 'politician'?" The answer can only be "No." Reform in its widest sense was undoubtedly the ideal Gregory set before himself — a reform of the whole of society was the thing which he most desired to see — but reform in the narrower sense was at most a part of his object; he was not concerned solely with the condition of the Church in the sense of an ecclesiastical organisation, and was not opposed only to monarchy if — or because — monarchy prevented the eradication of abuses. The theory that Gregory set out to establish the primacy of Rome because the weakness of the Church had led to its "enslavement" by temporal princes, whose control had in turn resulted in simony and nicolaitism — so that from an attack on simony and clerical incontinence the rest of the Gregorian programme follows logically — is attractively simple, but it quite fails to do justice to Gregory. He was indeed deeply concerned about simony and the marriage of priests, but these things were not the core of the movement to which he has given his name, nor the explanation of the struggle with kings and emperors. If it is true, as we have said, that the real issue was the establishment of the "right order in the world," and if this meant the supremacy of priests over laymen — and the supremacy of the pope in particular, as the chief of all priests — then one conclusion alone can follow: Whether the results of royal control were good (as they were under Henry III), or bad (as they may be admitted to have been under Henry IV), it still remained true that, for Gregory, royal control was in itself an evil. There could be no compromise on this principle, though doubtless there had to be *de facto* compromises in certain cases, like that of William the Conqueror.

This analysis shows how truly Gregory VII deserves to be called "the great Innovator"; his outstanding quality was his ability clearly and directly to assert first principles and to apply them to the practical requirements of the situation in which he found himself. At the same time, the fundamental importance of Professor Tellenbach's careful distinction between Gregory and his supposed precursors is revealed: only such a distinction brings to light the essential novelty of Gregory's position — which is otherwise in danger of being obscured in the shadows cast by the great reforming movements which preceded him — and throws his real greatness into bold relief.

In what sense may we speak of the "novelty" of Gregory's position? The following pages will make it clear that there was in his programme a relatively small proportion of new ideas; there were precedents for most of Gregory's actions, and all arguments to the contrary must fail. Gregory drew upon tradition, yet made a new use of it. He took the oldest of traditions — that of the Catholic Church, with the irrefutable claims its sacramental doctrines gave to the demand of the priesthood that their supremacy should be recognized — and showed how no true Catholic could resist the entirely novel construction he placed upon it. While there are strong reasons for denying that, at the time of the synod of Sutri, for instance, the alliance of the monarchy with reform was already foredoomed to turn into opposition, a more wide-ranging view must reveal the truth of the assertion that the dogmatic structure of the early Church made the emergence of the Gregorian programme a logical necessity. Gregory was the completest and most ruthless Catholic who had yet held office in the Church, and yet he was a revolutionary; innovation and an obstinate refusal to abate one jot or tittle of the law met in him to form a paradoxical and yet entirely consistent whole.

Gregory attained a very considerable measure of success, but his victory was far from complete. During his pontificate, we have said, the Church finally abandoned the old attitude of withdrawal and turned to attempt the conversion of the world; in spite of this, however, the old outlook persisted: the next century saw a monastic revival on a hitherto unprecedented scale, and generations of historians have agreed in awarding to St. Bernard, its leading figure, the title of "the ideal monk" — in describing him, that is to say, as the chief exponent of some of the ideas against which Gregory VII had fought. So, too, it proved impossible to confine the laity to a purely passive rôle in Church matters, because more settled and more prosperous conditions gave many of them leisure to ponder upon spiritual truth, and led to the conclusion that all men were called to play an equal part in religious activity. Accordingly, the twelfth and thirteenth centuries saw a wide development of popular religion, which frequently ended in heresy and was often tainted with anti-sacerdotalism; and this last is, of course, no less than a denial of the sacramental principles for which Gregory stood and upon which the subordinate position assigned to the laity was based. Even when the "conversion" *motif* appeared again with new force in the mendicant movements of St. Francis and St. Dominic, it was in the end unable to deal effectively with the problem of the layman's religion. Finally, despite the creation of a papal monarchy in the thirteenth and fourteenth centuries, the "national church" tendency persisted with undiminished force; Divine Right itself lasted many hundred years more — the long continuance of the practice of touching for the King's Evil shows how difficult it was to eradicate the feeling that the king was more than an ordinary layman — while the reign of Philip the Fair, the Gallican movement and the concordats of the fifteenth century, for instance, show that princely control of the Church had lost little of its theocratic dress, if it was also beginning to clothe itself in a more secular garb and to appeal to expediency and the new conception of the sovereign State.

For a short time, Gregorianism may have conquered both Church and World, but from early in the thirteenth century at latest the old tendencies of episcopalism, nonresistance and royal control raised their heads again. If the lessons taught by the conflict of ideals in the Investiture Contest of the eleventh century are of permanent value to a world which aspires to arrange its affairs according to Christian principles, it is equally clear that contemporary society failed properly to learn them; and this failure in its turn — at least in so far as its unintended effect was to drive the papal monarchy to an ever more intransigent assertion of its authority, and in the end to separate it from the religion of the world which it set out to convert — was in some way responsible for the occurrence of the next great crisis in Christian history, the Reformation.

MONASTIC REFORM
AND CHRISTIAN CULTURE

CHRISTOPHER DAWSON

Professor Dawson was educated at Trinity College, Oxford, and has devoted a long career and many volumes to the study of civilization, emphasizing
mediaeval Christian European civilization. He has filled many important lec-
tureships and was Gifford Lecturer in 1947–1948. From 1958 to 1960, Dr.
Dawson was professor of Roman Catholic Studies at Harvard Divinity School.
The selection taken from his Gifford Lectures, *Religion and the Rise of Western
Culture*, perhaps may be considered deficient in its treatment of the political
intricacies of the period under study, but it has the merit of emphasizing the
religious basis of the reform of the church. Dr. Dawson's insistence on the
theological motivation of Humbert of Silva Candida's position and the biblical
basis of Gregory VII's zeal well illustrate an epoch filled with revolutionary
actions launched from a religious base. The over-all result, Dawson finds, is
an invigorated reformed Roman papacy furnished *in reality* with the universal
direction of western society: a direction Charlemagne had exercised but which
a Henry IV or Henry V could only claim to exercise.

A new movement arose from the midst of the feudal society to meet the new danger of the feudal secularization of the Church.

This movement was at first purely mo-nastic and ascetic. It took the form of a flight from the world and public life to the desert and the cloister, a repetition in different circumstances of the first great movement of Western monasticism which I described in earlier chapters.

For while the ecclesiastical hierarchy and the territorial Church in general were so much a part of contemporary society that they were almost at the mercy of the predominant social forces, the monastic in-stitution represented the principle of an au-tonomous Christian order which proved to be the seed of a new life for the whole Church. It is true that the old Carolingian monasteries had been exploited and secu-larized in the same way as the bishoprics,

but every monastery was an independent organism, and thus each new foundation provided the opportunity for a fresh start and a return to the observance of the Bene-dictine Rule which remained the conse-crated norm of monastic life.

Hence it was in the new monasteries founded by feudal princes or converted nobles, like Cluny in Burgundy (910), Brogne and Gorze in Lorraine and Camal-doli in Tuscany (1009), that the founda-tions were laid of the new movement of spiritual reform that was to transform the medieval Church.

No doubt the monk was concerned pri-marily with the salvation of his own soul rather than with any programme of ecclesi-astical reform. But as we have seen, West-ern monasticism always possessed a strong consciousness of its social responsibility and its missionary functions. If on the one hand it was based on the tradition of the

Reprinted from *Religion and the Rise of Western Culture* by Christopher Dawson — By permission
of the Society of Authors and Mr. Christopher Dawson.

Fathers of the Desert, it was inspired still more by the ideals of St. Augustine and St. Gregory. The Augustinian theology and philosophy of history with their intense realization of the burden of inherited evil under which the human race laboured and their conception of divine grace as a continually renewed source of supernatural energy which transforms human nature and changes the course of history — all this had become part of the spiritual patrimony of the Western Church and, above all, of Western monasticism, and Christendom had only to return to this tradition to recover its dynamic energy.

Thus although the efforts of the reformers of the tenth century were primarily devoted to the cause of monastic reform, they involved far wider issues. These men were not mere self-centered ascetics, but prophets of righteousness who defended the weak and the oppressed and spoke boldly against evil in high places. We see this, above all, in the writings of St. Odo, the second Abbot of Cluny (927–942), who was one of the greatest of the early leaders in the reforming movement. . . .

But St. Odo realizes that this reign of injustice has its roots deep in human nature and cannot be abolished by reliance on external means — on "the arm of the flesh." From the days of Abel, the first of the just, down to the last of the elect, suffering and defeat have been the portion of the children of God. The only remedy is to be found in that spiritual force by which the humility of God conquers the pride of the evil one. Hence the spiritual reformer cannot expect to have the majority on his side. He must be prepared to stand alone like Ezekiel and Jeremy. He must take as his example St. Augustine besieged by the Vandals at Hippo, or St. Gregory preaching at Rome with the Lombards at the gates. For the true helpers of the world are the poor in spirit, the men who bear the sign of the cross on their foreheads, who refuse to be overcome by the triumph of injustice and put their sole trust in the salvation of God.

To the modern this may appear an unpractical conclusion. Nevertheless it undoubtedly gave spiritual force to the movement of reform which the Carolingian Church had looked for in vain from councils and kings. However good were the intentions of the latter, they seldom had the power to give effect to their resolutions. The monastic reform, on the other hand, was an autonomous movement which derived its power from its internal spiritual resources. It was assisted rather than hindered by the decentralization and local particularism of the feudal society, for these conditions made it possible for a founder to establish his new religious foundation without the interference of king or bishop. The classical example of this is Cluny itself, which was founded by Count William of Auvergne in 910 as the property of the apostles in immediate dependence on the Holy See, formally excluding any intervention whatsoever by king, bishop or court — a privilege which became the pattern and ideal for the other reformed monasteries. Thus from the beginning a kind of alliance was established between the Papacy and the monastic reformers, an alliance which was already confirmed by St. Odo's relations with Alberic, the Roman prince, and Leo VII in the first half of the tenth century.

Moreover the loose and shapeless organization of the feudal state made it possible for the reformed congregations to extend their influence by patronage and recommendation in the same way as a great feudal estate, so that a reformer like St. Abbo of Fleury could even say in jest that he was more powerful than the king of the Franks since his abbey possessed dependencies in lands where the king had no authority.

But though the influence of Cluny extended from Southern Italy to Eastern England it was by no means the only centre of reform. A similar movement was arising about the same time in the Low Countries where St. Gerard of Brogne (d. 959) was the reformer of the chief monasteries of Flanders, St. Peter and St. Bavo at Ghent,

St. Omer, St. Bertin and St. Ghislain, and somewhat later a group of clerks from Metz established an equally important centre at Gorze in Lorraine under St. John of Vandières. In Italy the tradition of the monks of the desert and the oriental anchorites was revived by the action of ascetics like St. Nilus, the Byzantine monk, who founded the great Basilian monastery of Grottaferrata south of Rome, St. Romuald, the founder of Camaldoli, and St. John Gualbert, the founder of Vallombrosa. . . .

Thus all over Europe new centers of monastic reform were arising like islands of peace and spiritual order in the sea of feudal anarchy. Monasticism had ceased to be a helpless spectator of the moral disorder of Christendom, and had become an independent power in Western society. In men such as St. Odo and St. Romuald and St. William of Volpiano the lawless feudal nobles, who cared nothing for morality or law, recognized the presence of something stronger than brute force — a numinous supernatural power they dared not ignore. St. Peter Damian records that Ranier, the Marquis of Tuscany, used to say that no emperor could put such fear into him as a mere glance of St. Romuald, and even after his death the saint was still regarded as the protector of the poor and the avenger of the oppressed. . . .

By the beginning of the eleventh century the movement of monastic reform had attained maturity and began to affect every aspect of Western culture. The great abbots who were the leaders of the movement, like St. Odilo of Cluny (994–1019), St. Abbo of Fleury (988–1004), St. Poppo of Stavelot (977–1048), and St. William of Volpiano (990–1031), were the dominant figures of the age and exercised immense influence on contemporary rulers. Never had the movement for the foundation and restoration of monasteries been more active than, for instance, in Normandy, where the foundations of this age, like Fécamp and

Bec and St. Evroult, became the centres of a great revival of Christian culture.

Nevertheless the reformers had as yet no idea of any fundamental change in the relations between the spiritual and temporal power. They still accepted the traditional Carolingian conception of the divine right of kings and the duty of the prince to intervene in religious and ecclesiastical affairs. In so far as they were concerned with the state of the Church outside the monastery, it was to the royal power rather than to the bishops or the Papacy that they looked for support. We see this clearly in the writings of the leading canonists of the time, like St. Abbo of Fleury and Bishop Burchard of Worms. The work of the former is addressed expressly to the French king, Hugh Capet, and his successor Robert the Pious, whose power he regarded as a sacred ministerial office for the rule and the reform of the Church; while the latter in his great *Decretum* represents the tradition of the bishops of the Empire and accepts the authority of the Emperor in the government of the Church without any consciousness of the contradiction between this state of affairs and the traditional principles of Canon Law on which his work is based.

However inconsistent this attitude might be, it corresponded with the facts of the situation. For the movement for the restoration of ecclesiastical discipline and canonical order during the early part of the eleventh century depended entirely on the sympathy and cooperation of the royal power. It was the Emperor rather than the Pope who took the initiative in the work of reform, and it was under the auspices of emperors like Henry II and kings of France like Robert the Pious that the first reforming councils and synods were held in Germany, Italy and France (e.g. at Pavia in 1022 and at Bourges in 1031).

But the exercise of the royal supremacy in religious matters was not conceived in any hostile spirit towards Rome. The relations between the Empire and the Papacy had never been more friendly and intimate than they were in the time of Otto III and Sylvester II in 999, and Henry II and Benedict VIII (1012–24).

So long, however, as the Papacy was under the control of the Roman nobility, its interests were limited by the feuds of local factions; and so far from taking the lead in the movement of reform, it was in dire need of reform itself. Throughout the tenth century the secularism and corruption of the rival cliques which exploited the Papacy were a flagrant denial of the ideals of the reforming movement, and the reaction of the Northern episcopate found violent expression in the synods of St. Basle and Chelles in 991 and 995. The fact that the spokesman of this anti-Roman opposition, Gerbert, himself became Pope Sylvester II four years later provided an unexpected dénouement of the conflict; but after a generation, the worst scandals of the tenth century were revived by John XIX and Benedict IX. Finally the deposition of Benedict IX and the election of two rival candidates led to the decisive intervention of the Emperor Henry III, who at the Council of Sutri in 1046 set aside all three Popes and imposed a German bishop, Suiger of Bamberg, as his own nominee.

Henry III was an austere and devout man, a friend of saints and reformers, who took his theocratic responsibilities towards the Church very seriously. Consequently it is not surprising that his drastic action at Rome met with general approval from the reforming party, apart from one or two exceptions like Bishop Wazo of Liège. Even St. Peter Damian, the leader of the Italian reformers, accepts his control of the Papacy as a manifestation of Divine Providence, and he compares his reforming action to that of Christ driving the money-changers from the temple!

The action of Henry III had a far-reaching effect on the course of the reforming movement. At first sight it might seem that it would reduce the Papacy to complete dependence on the imperial power, for the three Popes whom he nominated in rapid succession — Clement II in 1046 and Damasus II and St. Leo IX in 1048 — were loyal prelates of the Empire from Germany and Lorraine, who had no Italian connections and were consequently forced to rely on the material support of the Emperor. Nevertheless, the mere fact that the Papacy was taken out of the control of the Roman nobles and their factions and brought into intimate relations with Northern and Central Europe had an immediate effect on its international influence.

Still more important was the fact that the coming of Leo IX created an alliance between the Papacy and the movement of religious reform, which had its centre in Lorraine and Burgundy. As Bishop of Toul, Leo had been for twenty-two years one of the leading figures in the Church of Lorraine at a time when it was the scene of the reforming activity of abbots like St. Richard of Verdun, St. Poppo of Stavelot and St. Odilo of Cluny, and of bishops like Wazo of Liège — all of whom died about the time when he became Pope. And the men whom he brought to Rome as his chosen helpers were all drawn from the same milieu — Humbert, the Abbot of Moyenmoutier, Hugh the White, Abbot of Remiremont, and Frederick, the Archdeacon of Liège, who was brother of Duke Godfrey of Lorraine and was later to become Abbot of Monte Cassino and Pope Stephen IX.

The introduction of this foreign element into the Curia had a revolutionary effect on the Papacy, which became the hierarchical centre and organ of leadership for the reforming movement. The reform of the Church was no longer the aim of scattered groups of ascetics and idealists, it became the official policy of the Roman Church.

In his brief pontificate of less than five years St. Leo devoted himself to the work of reform with superhuman energy, crossing the Alps again and again to hold reforming councils in Germany and France as well as in Italy, and established direct personal control over the Churches of

Western Christendom. At the same time he took an important part in the political affairs of Christendom. He had to deal with the difficult problem of the Normans, who were establishing themselves in Southern Italy with no less ruthlessness and violence than that of the Danes in England. He attempted to meet this danger by direct military action, supported by both the German and Byzantine Empires. But his well-planned political strategy met with military disaster. He was defeated and captured by the Normans, and at the same time his plan for union between Western Christendom and the Byzantine Empire was resisted by the ecclesiastical intransigence of the Byzantine patriarch Michael Cerularius. He did not survive these disasters, and two years later, in 1056, the Emperor Henry III died prematurely, leaving his five-year-old son to succeed him under the regency of his widow.

This event was fatal to the old order and put an end to the cooperation between the Empire and the Papacy on which the policy of the reformers had hitherto been based. During the minority of Henry IV, the party of reform asserted the independence of the Papacy, disregarded the concordat of Sutri and began to elect their own candidates to the Papacy in independence of the Empire. They allied themselves with the anti-imperial party in Italy, represented by Duke Godfrey of Lorraine and Tuscany whose brother Frederick of Lorraine became Pope Stephen IX in 1057. Finally, they brought about the alliance between the Papacy and the Normans in Southern Italy, a reversal of alliances which had enormous consequences, since it was an open defiance, not only of the German Empire, but of the Byzantine Empire also, and did more than anything else to make the breach with the Eastern Church irremediable.

The moving spirit behind these events seems to have been Humbert of Moyenmoutier, Cardinal Bishop of Silva Candida, who was the dominant figure alike in the reforming movement and in the negotiations with Constantinople and the Normans during these critical years (1049–61). The ideas which inspired his activity are to be seen in his treatise *Against the Simonists* (c. 1058), which is at once the earliest, the ablest, and the most extreme statement of the programme of the reformers. To Humbert, simony was not merely a sin; it was the supreme heresy, since it denied the spiritual character of the Church and subordinated the gifts of the Spirit to money and worldly power. But since the Holy Ghost cannot be bought or sold, it follows, so he argued, that the Simonists had no share in His gifts. Their sacraments were null and void, and their church was the church of Anti-Christ. To meet these evils he called for a return to the old canonical principles of free election and the emancipation of the Church from the control of the secular power and from the custom of lay investiture. Since the spiritual power is as superior to that of the king as heaven is superior to earth, the Church should guide and rule the state as the soul rules the body; so only was it possible to ensure the reign of justice and the peace and union of the Christian people.

It is clear that these views are irreconcilable, not only with the current practice and union of eleventh-century Feudalism, but with the whole tradition of the imperial state Church which had inextricably confused spiritual and secular functions, and had regarded emperors and kings as the divinely appointed leaders of Christian society. It was a reversion to the uncompromising dualism and anti-secularism of the early Church.

The revolutionary consequences of these theories were not clear to the older generation of reformers, who were Humbert's contemporaries, like St. Leo IX and the great leader of the monastic reform in Italy, St. Peter Damian, who remained faithful to the ideal of the union of the two powers which had been temporarily realized in the time of Henry III. But after the death of Cardinal Humbert and Pope Nicholas II in 1061 the leadership of the movement passed to younger men who were prepared to carry the ideas of Humbert to their logical conclusion at whatever cost. Foremost among them was the archdeacon of the Roman Church, the Tuscan Hildebrand, who had held an important position at Rome since 1059 and was elected Pope in 1073 as Gregory VII.

Although the importance of his influence on the history of medieval Christendom has always been fully recognized, his personality and his work have been the subject of the most diverse judgments. On the one hand, he has been regarded as the prime mover and inspirer of the whole reforming movement, and on the other as an ambitious ecclesiastical politician of the type of Boniface VIII. But it is now generally recognized that both these views are equally erroneous. He was not an original thinker, for it was not Hildebrand but Humbert of Moyenmoutier who was the theorist and ideologist of the reforming movement. But on the other hand he was no mere ecclesiastical power politician, but a man of intense spiritual convictions with a deep sense of his prophetic mission.

His view of the Church and the world was characterized by the same Augustinian dualism that we have seen in the case of St. Odo of Cluny, but this was the common tradition of the Church of his age, and there is much less trace of direct Augustinian influence in his writings than is to be found in the work of Cardinal Humbert. It is in the Bible and, above all, in the Prophets that the real source of Gregory VII's inspiration is to be found; and the primary scriptural doctrines of divine judgment, the divine law of justice and the prophetic mission provide the recurrent theme of all his thought and teaching. His sense of urgency of his mission and the terrible predicament of the Christian world finds its most striking expression in the last appeal he addressed to the Christian people from his exile in Salerno before his death. . . .

The Christian religion, the true faith taught to our fathers by the Son of God, has fallen so low that it is an object of scorn, not only to the Evil One, but even to the Jews, the Saracens and the pagans. These have laws that profit them not to salvation and yet they are faithful to them. But we, blinded by the love of the world, have forsaken the True Law.

Every day we see men who go to death in thousands for their lords or their fellows, but those who fear God, few as they are, think only of their own souls and forget their brethren.

Since the day when the Church has placed me on the apostolic throne, my whole desire and the end of all my striving has been that the Holy Church, the Bride of God, our mistress and our mother, should recover her honour and remain free and chaste and Catholic.

There is nothing political in this ideal of reformation. But the uncompromising simplicity with which it was formulated made it a revolutionary force in a world in which the Church had become a part of the social order, and ecclesiastical and political relations had become inextricably entangled. Above all, the old Byzantine and Carolingian ideal of the sacred monarchy was an obstacle to any radical programme of reform, since it consecrated the status quo and surrounded vested interests with the halo of sacred tradition. Hence Gregory VII's uncompromising determination to free the Church from its feudal dependence on the secular power meant the abandonment of the old Byzantine and Carolingian conception of the divine right of kings and the passive obedience of their Christian subjects. But since the reformers no less than the conservatives continued to accept the unitary character of Christian society, the denial of the imperial theocracy involved the assertion of the supremacy of the spiritual power in the social life of Christendom, so that it was inevitable that the Pope should take the place which the Emperor had hitherto occupied as the supreme leader and judge of the Christian people.

This change, revolutionary as it was, was in harmony with the changing conditions of the new age. The Empire was no longer able to fulfill even formally the universal functions which the Empire of Charlemagne had represented. It had become an archaic survival from the point of view of Western Europe as a whole, where the new feudal states had become the leaders of culture. Yet the sense of unity of Christendom was stronger than ever and demanded some new institutional expression, and the reformed Papacy provided such an expression more effectively than any political institution could have done, since it transcended national and territorial rivalries and possessed in the hierarchy and the Canon Law the necessary instruments for its realization. It was, moreover, far more flexible than the Empire, since it could create special forms of relations, not only with local churches and monasteries, but also with the territorial powers, in addition to its universal authority. Thus Gregory VII encouraged the rulers of the more remote Christian territories, such as Spain, Denmark, Hungary and Croatia, to accept the protection of the Holy See and become vassals of St. Peter. And though this did not imply any direct political control, it emphasized the new position of the Papacy as the centre of international society.

The new formulation of the theocratic idea was assimilated without great difficulty by the feudal society of the West, where the limitations of kingship were a matter of common experience. But it was a different matter in the Empire where the Carolingian tradition was so strong and where the Church and the bishops were the mainstay of the imperial system. Here there was a conflict of ideals as well as of social forces, and for generations Christendom was torn asunder by the conflict. For the first time in the history of the West an attempt was made to enlist public opinion on either side, and a war of treatises and pamphlets was carried on, in which the most fundamental questions concerning the relation of Church and state and the right of resistance to unjust authority were discussed exhaustively.

This marks a new departure in the history of Western culture, for it meant that men had begun to reason about the principles on which Christian society was based, and to use the appeal to these principles as a means of exchanging the existing order. When Gregory VII wrote, "The Lord says 'I am the Truth and the Life,' he did not say 'I am custom' but 'I am Truth'," he was invoking a new kind of Divine Right which was ultimately to prove stronger than the divine right of kings. . . .

By the Reformers the claim of the Emperor to dominate the Church is seen as another assault on the liberty of the City of God by the children of Babylon and the generation of Cain. To the Imperialists, on the other hand, the Reformers are the enemies of peace who destroy the unity of the one Body by separating the priesthood from the kingship, putting the weapons of carnal warfare in the hands of the Church. . . .

Since the Church was one, the Christian prince and the Emperor himself held his office within the Church, subject to the law of the Church and under the authority of its spiritual rulers. The temporal authority was therefore in a sense the authority of the Church in temporal affairs, exercised through its temporal ministers. And if these ministers went wrong it was the duty of the Church and of the Christian people to call them to order and, if necessary, to dismiss them in favour of a more suitable candidate. Stated in its extreme form, as in the *Letter to Gebhard* by Manegold of Lautenbach, this involves the substitution of an almost democratic theory of social contract for the traditional principle of the divine right of kings, as well as a drastic justification of the employment of force against schismatics and heretics, according to the words of the prophet "Cursed be he who doeth the work of the Lord negligently and cursed be he that keepeth back his sword from blood." That this was not a matter of abstract theory is shown by the history of the Saxon revolt, as recorded by Lambert of Hersfeld and Bruno of Magdeburg, both of whom stress the conditional character of the allegiance of the Saxons to the Emperor and the right and duty of defending their national liberties and those of the Church. . . .

And so, too, it was not the Empire but the reformed Papacy which was the real heir of the Roman tradition of universalism and international order. For the Church was not only a much more universal and comprehensive society than the mediaeval state; it exercised many of the functions which we regard as essentially political. As F. W. Maitland used to insist, it is impossible to frame any acceptable definition of the state which would not include the medieval Church. It was a sovereign power which imposed its own laws and enforced them in its own courts by its own judges and lawyers. It possessed an elaborate system of appellate jurisdiction, an organized bureaucracy and an efficient system of centralized control carried out by permanent officials and supervised by the visits and reports of the legates who played such a prominent part in the international life of Christendom.

All this was the direct outcome of the reforming movement, for the emancipation of the Papacy from its dependence on the Empire and the separation of the spiritual authority of the bishop from his secular obligations as a member of the feudal hierarchy made it necessary to reconstruct the whole order of ecclesiastical administration and jurisdiction as an organized unity.

THE INVESTITURE CONTEST AND THE GERMAN CONSTITUTION

GEOFFREY BARRACLOUGH

Among British scholars, few have published more fundamental analyses of the mediaeval papacy and the empire than Geoffrey Barraclough, Research Professor of International History at the University of London. After receiving his education and historical training at Oxford, the University of Munich, and the British School at Rome, his publications on the mediaeval papacy and empire were interrupted by World War II. After the war he held the professorship of mediaeval history at the University of Liverpool.

This selection from *The Origins of Modern Germany* (1948) places great emphasis on the evolution of the Germanic constitution. The internal struggles between the crown and the princes, the maneuvering for papal support, and the confusion in political theories, make for blurred image — blurred because Barraclough is dealing with extremely fluid materials. His evaluation of the imperial powers of Henry III contrasted with those of Henry V should be noted.

I

THE remarkable recovery of Germany under the Saxon and Salian emperors, achieved in large measure through the willing cooperation of kings and churchmen, had rescued the Church from the heavy hand of the lay princes and built up its power and wealth and influence. Rulers like Henry II and Henry III had unhesitatingly turned from the immediate task of preserving royal authority to the further tasks of reform and the propagation of Christian culture which were incumbent on a "just king." They had willingly used their royal authority for the benefit of the Church, never doubting that such a use of authority was, in the Church's eyes, "just" and "righteous." They had called on bishops and abbots to assist them in their task, and the clergy, impelled not merely by a sense of the solidarity of its own interest with those of the crown, but also and still more by a belief in the "justice" of the king's control of Church and State, had willingly cooperated. They had accepted the king as the divinely appointed "ruler" of the Church, as the *rex et sacerdos,* marked out by the sacred oil of unction as God's vicar on earth; and they looked to the monarch for leadership, and found in him a leader in the task of eradicating abuse and establishing a Christian Society.

Suddenly, in 1073, with the election of Gregory VII to the Holy See, this whole conception of the relationship of Church and State, and with it the whole existing scheme of society, was challenged. It was challenged in the name of reform by a papacy which set out (in the words of an Italian bishop of the period) to champion lost laws which should be revived, against customs which had become corruptions. Whether the needs of reform required a revolutionary attack on the existing social and political order is one of the eternally debatable questions of history.

Reprinted by permission from *The Origins of Modern Germany*, 2nd Ed., by Geoffrey Barraclough, pp. 101–134 (Oxford: Basil Blackwell, 1948).

There were, even among the most ardent reformers, many sincere and distinguished churchmen who were prepared to deny it and to oppose Gregory VII and his programme; they held that the Church's task was moral regeneration, not a re-ordering of the fundamental laws and principles of society, and on a lower and more practical plane they were unwilling to forgo the help which the monarchy could give to the reforming party. They appreciated the positive benefits of a strong monarchy in a corrupt, materialist society, and perceived that a major political conflict would compromise the true objects of reform. But the tide was against them, and when their leader, the great Peter Damiani, cardinal-bishop of Ostia, died in 1072, the Gregorian party won the upper hand. From the very beginning of his pontificate — indeed, from the remote days when he accompanied Pope Gregory VI into exile and when, under Alexander II (1061–1073), he became a more influential figure at the papal Curia than the pope himself — Gregory was a determined opponent of the German emperors, and seems to have made up his mind that the only way to bring the work of reform to completion was to overturn the old order, in which abuse and disorder had grown rife, and to remodel society on principles derived from a study of the old law and canons of the Church. Before he became pope, he urged Deusdedit and Damiani (and doubtless others) to search the libraries and bring together all decretals, canons and passages from historians setting forth the powers of the Holy See; after he became pope he distilled what he considered the essence of this research into twenty-seven propositions, famous as the *Dictatus papae*. Like all revolutionaries he convinced himself that he was only restoring the old law; but the principles he enunciated fell like a bombshell on the traditional thought of the age, which they challenged at every turn. Every sentence of the *Dictatus papae*, drawn up by Gregory in 1075, implies a programme; but none is more astounding than the curt statement that the pope may lawfully depose emperors. Gregory — "the great innovator, who stood quite alone" — was setting out on new and perilous paths.

After 1073, therefore, the political wing of the reform party assumed control. Many factors contributed to give it predominance, and thus to bring about open conflict with the empire. In the first place, we may recall the work of Henry III in freeing the papacy from the control of Roman factions and thus enabling it to resume its function as the head of an oecumenical church. The popes introduced by Henry restored the prestige of the papacy in Europe, and his support enabled them to extend their field of action. He deliberately made the papacy a fit instrument for carrying out the work of reform to which he was devoted, and through the popes appointed with his support he brought it into contact with the main currents of reform, which had sprung up, independent of the papacy, in the western fastnesses of his empire, in Burgundy and Lorraine. Through Leo IX (1049–1054) the reform movement of Cluny found its way to Rome — a movement which was already pursuing objects less exclusively religious than the regeneration of monastic life. The Cluniac aim of freeing the churches, particularly monastic churches from direct lay control — an aim expressed in the programme of "free election" — was soon merged in a policy of raising the standards of lay society itself, because it was evident that the freedom of religious houses from aristocratic exploitation and control could never be assured unless lay society itself were purified and the worst excesses of feudalism eradicated. Hence it was through the action of Cluniac abbots and bishops that the Truce of God, the "peace movement," was introduced at the end of the tenth century as a means of combatting feudal disorder which was particularly rampant in the old lands of the Middle kingdom, in Burgundy and Lorraine, where (in contrast with Germany) imperial rule was little more than nominal. The object was to establish a new, more peaceful social order, in which the "liberty" which the churches claimed would be secure; and in this sense there is at least an element of truth in the view that the Cluniac movement was from its inception, a political movement. But these political objectives did not involve hostility to the empire, or to the principles of imperial government, and it was only when Cluniac ideas and principles were adopted by the papacy and remoulded in combination with other elements of papal policy that the Cluniac movement and its off-shoots, of which the most important was Hirsau in southern Germany, became a formidable political power directed against the German monarchy. Under Gregory VII, although the leaders of the Cluniac movement still maintained a mediating position between pope and emperor, the monks and disciples of Cluny and Hirsau were the shock-troops of the papal army, the executants of papal orders, the protagonists of papal authority.

It was the pontificate of Leo IX (1049–1054) which saw the first rapid advance in the reconstruction of papal authority. Three times crossing the Alps to France and Germany, and holding synod after synod at which he legislated against abuse, Leo made the papal headship a reality. Already in 1049 at the synod of Reims he insisted on the requirement of canonical election to ecclesiastical offices. Everywhere he went he received the homage of bishops, thus demonstrating papal primacy in spite of the opposition of metropolitans, who refused to admit that the bishop of Rome had any right to interfere in the administration of their provinces. At the same time he gave the Roman Curia an international complexion corresponding to its oecumenic claims, by elevating non-Italians — chiefly his fellow-countrymen from Lorraine — to the cardinalate. Continuous control of the provinces was inaugurated by the frequent dispatch of cardinal-legates to inspect and reform,

while bishops were pressed to visit the Holy See. Thus the foundations of the papal monarchy were laid. But it was the radical change in the political situation after Henry III's death in 1056 which enabled the papacy to consolidate its position. The succession of a minor and the regency of the Empress Agnes immediately resulted in a disastrous weakening of German power in Italy, and although the papacy still had to contend with the Roman factions, which again began to raise their heads, and with Duke Godfrey of Lorraine, who threatened to enthral it, it was quick to profit from the change of circumstances. When the German pope, Victor II, the last of Henry III's candidates, died in 1057 and was replaced by Godfrey of Lorraine's brother, Stephen IX, the only acknowledgement of the old imperial right of confirmation was the dispatch to Germany of a belated embassy after the pope had already been consecrated. Two years later the procedure for papal elections was defined and remodelled, electoral rights being for practical purposes placed in the hands of the cardinals. This change was intended primarily to free the papacy from dependence on the Roman mob, which had intervened on the death of Stephen IX in 1058; but it could be, and was, used also against the emperor and the imperial government, whose rights were whittled away; for although a vague personal right of confirmation was reserved for Henry IV, it was rendered meaningless by a decision empowering the person elected to exercise all the prerogatives of pope from the moment of his election. Thus the choice of the pope was made the affair of the cardinals, who were already an international body with little sympathy for the German government. The danger was quickly perceived at the imperial court, and on the death of Pope Nicholas II in 1061 a last attempt was made to preserve imperial rights. Asked by the Roman nobles to nominate a successor, the empress designated Bishop Cadalus of Parma, who was elected by German and Lombard bishops at a synod at Basel; but in the meantime the reform party, without consulting the imperial government, had elected Bishop Anselm of Lucca, a protégé of Godfrey of Lorraine, as Alexander II. The result was a schism, which continued until Cadalus' death in 1072; but already by 1064 the course of events in Germany had broken imperial resistance. The abduction of Henry IV by the princes at Kaiserswert in 1062, and the collapse of the regency government brought new powers into the saddle: Anno of Cologne, the bitter opponent of Adalbert of Bremen and therefore of imperial policy, went over to the reform party and under his influence a synod held at Mantua in 1064 decided in favour of Alexander II.

Thus the minority of Henry IV and the weakness and embarrassments of the regency compromised German government to such a degree that the papacy was able to carry through a revolutionary reorganization almost without protest and to emancipate the Roman church from imperial and German influence. Deprived of effective imperial support the bishops of Germany and Lombardy were left to fight in isolation against the centralizing policy of the papacy which threatened to sweep away their privileges and independence. They saw themselves subjected to legates, who were sent out from Rome to enforce clerical celibacy and repress simony; and many of the most distinguished prelates, including Anno of Cologne himself, were summoned to Rome to answer for their actions. The Lateran Council of 1059 had attacked lay investiture, and the radical wing of the reform party already condemned all forms of lay investiture as simony, thus laying an axe at the roots of the established connexion between Church and State and at the system by which the monarchy, in Germany and in Lombardy, governed by entrusting counties and jurisdictions to carefully selected bishops. But conditions during Henry IV's minority were manifestly exceptional, and it was obvious that the papacy had to expect an

imperial attempt to recover its lost rights as soon as Henry IV was firmly established in the saddle. To meet this contingency it needed allies, just as it needed allies within the Church against the bishops, whom a very evident community of interests drove into the royal camp. The earliest, as we have seen, was Duke Godfrey of Lorraine, whose power in Tuscany was a constant though dangerous bulwark of the papacy, ever threatening to turn protection into domination. Equally dangerous was the alliance with the Normans, formed in 1059 at the very moment when Nicholas II's decree governing papal elections and the prohibition of lay investiture challenged the Germany monarchy. But both alliances helped the reform party to maintain its position, and it was the troops of Godfrey and the Normans which assured Alexander II's victory over his rival, Cadalus. In Germany, the papacy ever since the days of Leo IX had been in contact with the south German nobility, who saw in the reform programme — particularly in the demand for "free election" — a useful vehicle for the assertion of their rights against the centralizing policy of the monarchy. The German nobility, particularly in the west and in the south, quickly realized the advantages to be gained from support of the reform movement, and with their backing Cluniac influence spread with amazing rapidity during the decade following the introduction of Cluniac monks at St. Blasien in the Black Forest in 1060 and the reform of Hirsau about 1066. The result was the rapid propagation in Germany of a religious movement which owed its progress to the papacy and the princes, not to the empire, and which was organized with a maximum of cohesion since all new and reformed foundations received the status of priories, over which the abbot of Cluny retained control, without episcopal interference; for the papacy had granted Cluny exemption from the authority of any bishop save the bishop of Rome. This close-knit organization was of enormous advantage to the papacy. Dependent on papal prerogative for its autonomy, Cluny led the way in effective centralization in the western Church, and its monks were the best propagandists and champions of papal supremacy, particularly against the bishops who regarded the autonomy of the reformed monasteries as an encroachment on their canonical rights. Against the Lombard bishops, on the other hand, the papacy did not hesitate to ally with the social classes whose opposition to the episcopacy had introduced a new element of discord into Italian life during the past fifty or sixty years — an alliance with the "mob" which provoked violent disapproval. In Milan, in particular, the so-called "Patarini" stood out as champions of "free election," hoping to obtain the chief see of the north for one of their own number, and thus to secure greater power for the feudatories in the administration of Milanese fiefs and territories. Their alliance with and formal recognition by the papacy reached back to 1059, and the question of Milan, where a "Patarine" and an imperial bishop faced each other in bitter hostility, was the major issue between Henry IV and Gregory VII, after the latter's election to the Holy See in 1073. It was the test case which led to the outbreak of the conflict between Church and State.

The pontificate of Alexander II (1061–1073) represented, on the whole, a phase in which the reformers marked time. Much of it was taken up by the struggle with the anti-pope, Honorius II. At its close, the pope's Norman allies, after overrunning Apulia and Calabria, launched an attack on the papal territories, which temporarily estranged the two powers. There were difficulties also in Tuscany, where the younger Godfrey of Lorraine, who had married his stepsister, Matilda, was at loggerheads with his wife, and prepared to accept Henry IV's aid in recovering from her the Tuscan lands. Hence the position of the papacy, when Gregory VII was elected pope in 1073, was no longer strong and there was some possibility of a com-

promise. Gregory appears to have proceeded cautiously over his election, the validity of which was disputed by the German episcopate, and to have secured Henry's approbation by agreeing to postpone his ordination until royal confirmation had been received; and for some months longer he steered a moderate course, apparently seeking an understanding. Henry also, involved in the Saxon wars, was conciliatory, admitting that he had sold churches to unsuitable persons and laid hands on ecclesiastical property, and promising in future to observe the pope's precepts. He warmly received a papal embassy which appeared at Nürnberg in 1074, and agreed to dismiss five of his ministers who had been excommunicated by Alexander II for simony. Negotiations between pope and emperor continued through the summer and autumn of 1075, but gradually the complexion of affairs changed. Both sides appear to have been to blame for the deterioration which now set in. In December 1074, taking advantage of the disturbances in Saxony, Gregory forbade all married priests in Germany to perform the sacraments — a measure which stirred up wide unrest. In February 1075 he took the more decisive step of prohibiting lay investiture — a prohibition, the wording and implications of which were obscure, but which, issued at that juncture, was evidently a challenge to the monarchy. The coincidence between the rebellion of the Saxons and the prohibition of lay investiture was not accidental; Gregory's action was deliberately timed. On the other hand, Henry himself, once the Saxons had been defeated, threw off the mask, united his cause with that of the German bishops, whom the pope was threatening, and advanced to the defence of his position in Lombardy. Already before the death of Alexander II he had sought a solution of the Milan question by setting aside the two rival candidates and appointing and investing a third — much as Henry III had solved the Roman question in 1046 — but the new appointment was resisted by the "Patarini" who, with the pope's approval, elected a new candidate. The failure of this attempt at a compromise solution led Henry to more extreme measures. Because the royal demesnes in Italy had shrunk to negligible proportions, royal authority there, when the king was not present with an army, depended chiefly on the bishops and became null if he could not appoint his own men. In 1075 Henry decided to support his candidate with armed forces, which quelled the riots of the Pataria. At the same time he entered into negotiations with the Normans and prepared to restore Godfrey of Lorraine to his position in Tuscany. Gregory's answer was the famous letter of December 8th, 1075, summoning the king to penance and due subjection, and threatening him with the loss of his throne. The formulation some time in 1075 of the theses of the *Dictatus papae* is the best evidence that, on Gregory's side, an open conflict was neither unforeseen nor unpremeditated. With the issue of the admonition of December 8th it became a fact.

Henry IV's reply to the pope's letter of December 8th, 1075, was to call together the synod of Worms of January 27th, 1076, where the king (in his capacity of *Patricius urbis Romanae*) and the assembled bishops solemnly declared Gregory's election null and void, and called on him to abdicate. Thus began the chain of events which led to civil war in Germany. At the Lenten synod in Rome, Gregory replied to the synod of Worms by excommunicating Henry and suspending him from government. Henry followed with the excommunication of the pope in an assembly of German bishops held at Mainz on the feast of St. Peter and St. Paul. Then came the first defections of German clergy and laity from Henry, the junction of the south German and Saxon oppositions, and the forging of a connexion between both and the papacy. In October 1076 the king came face to face with the united opposition at the Diet of Tribur,

and was forced to accept its terms, namely to free himself from excommunication within four months on pain of loss of his crown, and meanwhile to accept his suspension and withdraw into private life until the pope's decision was made known. With this in view the princes invited the pope to Augsburg, and it was to avoid facing such an assembly of his enemies and opponents, which he fully realized would be fatal for his cause, that Henry decided to seek out the pope in Italy. There followed the famous journey to Canossa, the meeting with the pope, penance and absolution. But Henry's secret flight to Canossa, although a clever manoeuvre to divide the papal and the German opposition, was in the eyes of the princes a breach of his undertakings at Tribur; and this breach and their consequent deep distrust of Henry decided the princes to proceed to the last step. On March 13th, 1077, they met at Forchheim, the traditional Frankish meeting-place for royal elections, and elected a new king, Rudolf of Swabia. Germany was divided into two camps, and a long generation was to pass before even the bare essentials of peace and settled conditions returned. But what was destroyed in these years could never be restored: the whole of subsequent German history bears on it the marks of the conflicts which raged through Germany between 1075 and Henry IV's death in 1106.

II

What were the issues in the war between Gregory VII and Henry IV which broke out at the end of 1075? The conflict is traditionally known as the Investiture Contest; but this is neither a very accurate nor a very adequate description. The question of lay investiture had been an element in the reform programme since the publication of Humbert of Moyenmoutier's treatise *adversus Simoniacos* in 1058; but it only became a central theme some years after Gregory VII's death when the conflict over greater issues had exhausted all parties, when both sides knew that their more sweeping claims could never be realized, and when detailed analysis of the questions at stake had fixed investitures as an issue the solution of which would permit compromise and peace. Gregory VII himself, despite his prohibition of lay investiture in 1075, was scarcely irreconcilable in this respect; what he was really concerned to enforce was his conception of free, canonical election, and provided this was assured there is every reason to suppose that he would — at any rate during the first phase of the conflict, prior to his recognition of Rudolf of Swabia in 1080 — have sanctioned the principle of lay investiture. But to secure such a solution, the king would have had to agree to limit investiture to bishops and abbots already canonically elected, and probably also not to refuse investiture to such candidates, whether or not he regarded them as politically suitable for their offices. The issue of canonical election was, however, a more difficult matter; for election by the clergy and people — which was the current meaning in reforming circles of "free election" — opened the door wide to local influence and particularist interests, which both in Germany and in Lombardy were all too apt to be directed against the crown and royal policy. In the twelfth century a solution was found, both in Germany and in England, by admitting the legitimacy of elections "in the king's presence," thus allowing the king to bring influence to bear on the electors or their representatives; but this compromise was the result of long mediation, and for Henry IV, at the beginning of the conflict, to have accepted "canonical election" in the sense of Gregory VII would have been tantamount to abandoning political control of the German and Lombard churches. Moreover, we must remember the atmosphere of suspicion engendered by reforming propaganda and by extreme elements, which were even more radical than the pope. The new and formidable connotation of the word "simony," which stigmatized all forms of lay

investiture as equivalent to traffic in the holy sacraments, was not calculated to appease the emperor; nor was the widely propagated view that there was no distinction between the church itself, the spiritualities, and its secular rights and properties. The specious argument that what had once been given to the church had been given to Christ in perpetuity, and that the donor had no further rights in his gift, was attractive; but it simply swept aside the fact, of which moderate churchmen like Cardinal Damiani were well aware, that apart from the gifts of the faithful most, if not all, great churches held estates which were not gifts but territories conceded for administration and political control. The churchmen who regarded the counties they held as so much property belonging to their churches, were deliberately or unconsciously confusing the issue; the county was a secular office with lands attached, and as such was properly conferred by lay investiture. Nor could the crown afford to see its control of the counties broken. In Lombardy, as we have seen, it was completely dependent on the bishops, who had largely engrossed the county organization; in Germany, it has been calculated that by 1073 no less than fifty-three counties were in the possession of the episcopate. In these circumstances Henry IV, in any compromise, required specific assurances guaranteeing his just interests, and no firm assurance was forthcoming: there was room for a compromise to get rid of the undoubted abuses of the existing system, but Henry could not throw the system over. Its maintenance was, for the German monarchy — which had only just begun to construct new foundations for its power — a matter of life and death.

It was, however, against the current system, and not simply against its abuse, that the Gregorian attack was launched. Henry was unscrupulous and untrustworthy in political dealings, a born tactician for whom the end justified the means; but it would be unwarranted to assume that he was fundamentally hostile to reform. There is no reason to doubt his sincerity when in 1082 he forswore simony; and it is significant that his antipope, Clement III, stood out in the cause of clerical celibacy in 1083 at the very moment when Gregory VII, owing to the adverse situation in which he found himself, had begun to waver. If the issue between Henry IV and Gregory VII had been merely traffic in Church dignities and the celibacy of the priesthood, the rupture between emperor and pope would probably never have occurred. The contest was not merely a fight between zealous reformers and vested interests; on the contrary one of the main arguments against Gregory was that he was destroying the "right order" of the Church, and the anti-Gregorians were as insistent as Gregory on the "justice" and rightness of their standpoint. Nor were the twin problems of investiture and canonical election, important as they were in practical politics, more than side-issues, significant mainly as the expression of more fundamental divergencies. What was at issue was the whole accepted and time-hallowed position of the Salian monarchy. Gregory VII attacked root and branch the ideas of legitimacy, divine right and paramount overlordship, on which the claim of the Salians to rule the German Church was founded. The reformed papacy could compromise with the Capetian and Anglo-Norman monarchies, but the theocracy of the Salians had to be eradicated because it was so mighty that it endangered the supremacy of Rome over the other Churches of Christian Europe. It was because the German Church, as reformed by Henry II and Henry III, was the least undisciplined Church in eleventh-century Europe that it was attacked; reform which was directed by the crown and which, if successfully continued, would have strengthened the attachment of the German Church to the crown, did not suit the papacy. An attack on the Salian monarchy was necessary for the emancipation of the papacy from the imperial system built up by Henry III. It was necessary because of the connexion between Germany and Italy, which now became a funereal entanglement involving the German ruler in an out-and-out war which he might otherwise have escaped. And it was necessary, finally, if the papal headship of the Church, which was the ultimate object of Gregorian policy, was to be a reality. So long as the king was (as Henry III had been called) *caput ecclesiae,* standing above all mortals in virtue of the holy right of unction, the representative on earth of "the highest Lord," the allegiance of the bishops was likely to remain divided, particularly as most of them, rightly or wrongly, regarded the pope's monarchical pretensions as a revolutionary attack on the canonically ordained order of the Church. A kingship with sacerdotal qualities, a ruler who was *rex et sacerdos,* was a natural rallying-point for ecclesiastical resistance; and on the king's side was tradition and fervent conviction as well as political expediency.

Fundamentally, therefore, the contest between Gregory VII and Henry IV centred round the monarchy and its place in Christian society. It was an issue with the widest ramifications, reaching out into all spheres of social and political life, and in the struggle which ensued the monarchists were the conservative, the Gregorians the revolutionary party. Gregory took up arms against the very conception of monarchy by divine right. Turning its back on the old Gelasian theory of the harmonious cooperation of the two great powers, the Hildebrandine party sought a separation of Church and State, involving a complete change in the position of the king in Christian society. It did not necessarily mean his subordination to the pope, although Gregory soon drew this positive conclusion from his own arguments; but it did mean necessarily that the king's sacerdotal position and character were challenged. For Gregory, the king was a removable official. He had a divine duty on earth; but he only remained king so long as he performed this duty, and if he ceased to act righteously he became *ipso facto* a tyrant, to whom no obedience was owed. Furthermore, it rested with the pope, as successor of Peter and vicar of Christ, to determine when a ruler was acting as a *rex iustus,* when he was a tyrant who must be removed. Rejecting the ancient doctrine that kings were sent by God, either as leaders of the righteous or as a scourge for the wicked, Gregory turned his back on the Christian dogmas of passive obedience and non-resistance. One of the most penetrating of Gregory's critics picked out the essential novelty of the pope's position, when he wrote: "Christ alone, in unison with God, can give or take away dominion, according to the scriptures; but Hildebrand teaches that he himself has authority over kings and kingdoms, and can do that which, according to the Psalmist, can be done by God alone, who abases the one and elevates the other." And Henry IV himself laid his finger on the main point: "You have dared," he wrote to Gregory, "to touch me, who although unworthy have been singled out by unction to rule, and whom, according to the traditions of the Holy Fathers, God alone can judge." But Gregory denied that unction conferred on the king a sacred character, which marked him out above men as God's anointed. "Aut rex est laicus, aut clericus," it was said; and thereby the whole earlier construction, in which the king's position was that of *rex et sacerdos,* priest as well as layman, was ridiculed. A good king could still serve the Church; but he was a subordinate serving a master, a warrior using his sword at the pope's behest. Moreover, because his position was that of an officer, he must be chosen as a lord would choose a bailiff. Not God's will, inscrutably manifest in the virtues of royal blood, was to decide who should rule, but practical tests of suitability. Suitability, *idoneitas,* was the test of kingship in Gregory's eyes; and it was the task of the lay princes to select and put forward for papal approval a candidate whose suitability was proven. The king's position in relation to the pope was, in short, to be the same as that which Gregory himself was striving to establish between pope and bishops. Like the bishops the king was to be freely elected, and the election was to be referred to the pope for confirmation. Like the bishops the king was to be chosen from below, he was to be the nominee of those over whom he was to rule, and not God's vicar, ruling by the grace of God and marked out for government by hereditary succession. For hereditary succession gave no guarantee of *idoneitas;* on the contrary, as Innocent III was later to affirm, it was a presumption against suitability. Gregory's theories of kingship therefore culminated in the political sphere, in a theory of election and of elective monarchy, which was the logical counterpart of his theory of monarchy as an office. The elective factor, which in Germany and the empire had retained only symbolic or formal significance, was thus revived and given new content. Hitherto the *electio* of which chroniclers speak had been the acclamation of an already designated king: henceforward it was to become election in the technical sense. Therewith it was implied that the real source of authority in the kingdom lay in the princes who elected the king. In the pope's view, the princes, not the king, were the representatives of the kingdom: king and kingdom were no longer (in the phrase of a seventeenth-century Englishman) "one creature, not to be separate in their political capacity." Clerical theory, as developed by the Hildebrandine party in the Investiture Contest, introduced an antagonism between king and kingdom, which in course of time found its culmination in the "dualism" of the period of representative estates, and led to the establishment of a political order in which the king, with his royal rights, stood opposed to the princes, who represented — or claimed to represent — the interests of the kingdom against the king.

Contemporaries had no illusions about

the revolutionary nature of Gregorian claims, the revolutionary character of the Gregorian movement, and the fact that Gregory himself often shrank abashed and hesitant from the practical consequences of his doctrines does not prove them wrong. The long period of hesitation before he recognized Rudolf of Swabia as king, the care with which for three whole years between 1077 and 1080 he addressed Henry as king and Rudolf only as pretendant, his denial that he had any share in Rudolf's election, testify to his scruples and to his persistent hopes of a reconciliation, on his own terms, with Henry IV. The fact remains that he threw a flaming brand into Germany, and that his hesitation and scrupulousness, although certainly dictated by honourable motives, not only sowed dissension among his supporters but also prolonged the social upheavals and thus added to the horrors of a bitter civil war. On all sides there were denunciations of Gregory's monstrousness in dissolving the bonds which held society together, and in handing over Germany to violence and anarchy. His deposition of Henry IV in 1076 was attacked both as an unheard-of assumption of power, and for its disastrous political effects. In the eyes of many, Gregory was simply a *destructor regni*, a fomenter of civil strife, and even his supporters warned him that in deposing Henry he was placing an insuperable obstacle in the path of his own adherents. "It is a novelty, unknown in any past age," wrote Wenrich of Trier, "for priests so easily to bring nations into civil strife, by a sudden act to shatter the name of king, which was discovered at the creation of the world and established by God, contemptuously to dismiss the Lord's anointed as if he were a mere bailiff, and to lay him under anathema if he does not instantly obey the command to abandon the kingdom of his fathers." Other writers condemned Gregory for "resisting the ordinance of God," and "destroying and bringing to naught the two powers by which the world is ruled."

Henry IV's own letters are full of the same charge. "Contrary to God's ordinance," he writes, "Gregory wishes to be king and priest at once; he wishes to discredit the king's sacred dignity, which derives from God and can only be taken away by God." The "Hildebrandine madness," he told the bishops in 1076, was confounding God's ordinance; he ruled by God's grace and not by the pope's grace, yet Gregory, who had no hand in raising him to the throne, was proposing to deprive him of his kingdom. God had set up two powers, but Gregory was attempting to reduce the two to one, and they who, as servants, of God, ought to have no part in worldly business, were taking it upon themselves to rule and govern kingdoms. Moreover, Gregory's inordinate ambitions were rending the body of Germany. Large parts of Saxony were uninhabited save for the beasts of the forests; civil strife was dividing families. Gregory, Henry said, was raising sons against fathers and arming brothers against brothers, and Berthold of Zwiefalten, described how "no man knew when his own father or son or brother might not bring death or ruin upon him." Right or wrong in principle, Gregory was doing irreparable damage.

The opponents of Gregory VII had at their backs the massive weight of conservative opinion; and it was to the traditional sentiments of the conservative masses that Henry IV again and again issued his stirring appeals. On the other hand, the Gregorian theories derived strength not only from their acceptance in reforming circles, but also from the fact that they fitted in with German political beliefs, which postulated that government was based on a pact, and that no king could continue to rule unless he observed the implicit conditions under which he was raised to the throne. Hence writers were not lacking who were prepared to argue that, even apart from the judgement of the Holy See, Henry had forfeited his title to the crown. For those whose sentiments these writers represented, Gregory was a welcome ally and Gregorian theories were a useful supplement to their own political arguments; for, where German political convictions justified revolt and self-help against a king who failed to observe and maintain the rights of his subjects, Gregorian theory provided a formal method of getting rid of such a king by means of judicial proceedings which stripped the king of his rights and released his subjects from allegiance. The vigorous but inchoate right to resist an unjust king, to which free German society was peculiarly sensitive because it had never experienced the full rigour of subjection to a feudal monarchy, was thus given a new lease of life and more precise political formulation when it came into contact with the ecclesiastical theories represented by Gregory VII; it thereby became a dominant principle in German political life at the very moment when elsewhere in western Europe it was being slowly but surely eradicated by the assertion of the king's prerogatives as feudal superior. For Gregory, on the other hand, the existence within Germany of a body of thought not far removed in spirit from his own, was an essential factor in winning popular support for his theories of monarchy and his attacks on the Salian dynasty and its principles of government. Nevertheless, the alliance between Gregory and the German opposition represented an accommodation of interests and not an identity of views; and as early as 1077, when the princes insisted on electing a new king, while the pope looked forward to the restoration of a penitent Henry, it became evident that the paths pursued by the princes and the papacy did not run parallel. For Gregory, the object was to secure Henry's adhesion to his own view of the place of the monarchy in Christian society; for the princes it was a case of seizing, before it was too late, the opportunity provided by the pope's suspension of Henry to get rid of a king whose policy threatened their interests and prerogatives.

Behind all the resounding appeals to principle, therefore, we must take into account the play and cross-currents of political interests. The opponents of Henry were a motley crowd, pursuing divergent interests; and it required all the efforts of the pope and his legates to hold them together. Gregory was not fastidious in his choice of allies. Unlike the earlier reforming popes, from Leo IX to his own immediate predecessor, Alexander II, he was not by birth a member of the episcopal aristocracy, and this was probably one reason why he did not hesitate to enlist the people and stir up popular discontent both in Germany and Italy. His alliance with the Pataria and the nascent communes in Lombardy brought him into disrepute; but he showed no hesitation in allying with forces which were seeking to revolutionize the existing order for secular ends. He appeared to throw over principle in favour of expediency when, in order to find a safe refuge at the moment of Henry IV's triumph, he came to terms with the Norman prince, Robert Guiscard, who had been excommunicated for occupying papal territory. His alliance with the German aristocracy was hard to justify save on political grounds; for its leaders were notorious despoilers of the Church, and the civil war unleashed by the excommunication of Henry in 1076 resulted in unparalleled depredation, of which Gregory himself was well aware as early as 1078. By his alliance with the German aristocracy Gregory sacrificed the prospect of lasting reform; for reform, in the eyes of the German princes, was little more than a pretext — as once again in the sixteenth century it was to be a pretext — to enable them to establish control over the Church. It is difficult to escape the conclusion that, for Gregory and his successors, the end justified the means, and that they were more intent on breaking the power of the crown within the Church than on purifying the Church from abuse. In this the Gregorian party was at loggerheads with the moderate party within the Church, the party led by Peter Damiani, which held that the movement against lay investiture was a false step which fatally distracted attention from the main task, the moral regeneration of the Church, and that cooperation with the monarchy was not impossible. For the Gregorians, on the other hand, the political struggle with the German monarchy overshadowed all else; and in this struggle they were willing to ally indiscriminately with princes, Saxons, Normans, communes and Pataria. In this sense the Gregorian movement was a truly revolutionary movement; just as its ultimate object was to overturn the accepted order, so its instruments and methods and alliances and associations were revolutionary in character. For the attack on the Salian monarchy and its principles of government, the papacy mobilized every revolutionary force within the empire: hence the unparalleled fury when the cataclysm was, at last, let loose.

III

The historical significance of Henry IV's reign lies in his resolute defence of the traditional rights of the monarchy against the attack led by Gregory VII. From his earliest manifesto at Worms in January 1076, he stands out in defence of his inheritance, the hereditary monarchy, the monarchy by divine right, the monarchy which is consecrated like the priestly office, the fate of which is beyond the touch of man and confided to God alone. "He began his reign," it has been well said, "as a revolutionary, attacking the old constitution: he finished as its last and almost its sole defender." His object is clear throughout, and he pursued it with amazing tenacity, turning first one way, then the next, without scruple or hesitation to secure any and every tactical advantage. He was quick to perceive and adept at exploiting every favourable circumstance, and for this reason it is not always easy to appreciate the logic of his policy. On the whole it is safe to say that he sought, so far as he was able, to come to terms with the Church in order to gain

a free hand to deal with the aristocracy, whose pretensions constituted in his eyes the most serious threat to the monarchy; but this policy, forced on him by circumstances, had strict limits, and he was never prepared, even at the moments of greatest crisis, to accept the Gregorian programme, which would have destroyed his political hold over the bishoprics of Germany and Lombardy and forfeited the support of the German episcopacy. What he saw, above all else, was that the only method of defending the traditional rights of the monarchy was to exploit to the full the divisions and divergencies of object and interests in the ranks of his opponents, and as time passed to profit from the general reaction against the excesses of the rebels; for the very arrogance of the coalition between pope and princes, and the anarchy into which it plunged Germany, had the unsought-for result of endowing the royalist cause with a new lease of popularity. In the measure in which Henry IV was successful, his success was due to the response his policy found in Germany, which was worn out by the long struggle and acutely perceived the situation to which the weakening of the monarchy was leading. Behind his conception of the kingship as something beyond the reach of the princes was a mighty force of ancient tradition, strongly rooted in German soil; and building on this strength Henry IV was at least able to maintain the old doctrine of hereditary monarchy. The principle of elective monarchy, enunciated at the election of the anti-king, Rudolf of Rheinfelden, in 1077, failed through Henry's efforts to find an immediate place in the constitution. He handed on the ancient theory of hereditary monarchy as an inheritance to his son, and the Hohenstaufen took it over from Henry V and defended it with new weapons. Only some two centuries after the election of Rudolf of Rheinfelden, in circumstances very different, did the view finally become prevalent that the German kingdom was an elective monarchy.

The Diet of Tribur, which met in October 1076 and sealed the alliance between the German princes and the papacy, first revealed the full dangers of Henry's position and the consolidation of the opposition to the Salian monarchy. Its prolonged deliberations appeared to spell the doom of the monarchy, but they also revealed the divergencies between the various elements which made up the opposition. Henry immediately used all his political skill to prise apart the united front. He played on the fact that only one section of the princes sought to depose him; the more moderate party, on the other hand, still hoped to retain him on the throne after he had purged himself and moderated his policy. He was well aware of the divergencies between the free peasantry and the nobility in Saxony, and the lukewarmness of the former who, after the failure of the revolt of 1073, came to realize that they were little more than pawns in the calculations of the princes. Even in reforming circles, he had adherents — led by the great abbot, Hugh of Cluny, whose reputation and moral stature were equal to the pope's — who were radically opposed to the attempt to exploit his conflict with Gregory in order to abase the monarchy. But above all else he realized the extent of the divergence of aims between Gregory, whose first object was to secure acceptance of the programme of canonical election, and the princes who thought first and foremost of undermining the centralizing policy of the Salian dynasty. His first success, exploiting these differences, was to secure a postponement of any decision until after a second meeting had been held at Augsburg, at which Gregory was to preside. But he carefully refrained from any specific engagement to attend or accept the decisions of the proposed Augsburg meeting. His second success was in avoiding any undertaking to surrender his rights over the Church. He promised Gregory due obedience and satisfaction; he accepted personal abasement and humiliation; but he surrendered nothing of the inherited rights of the monarchy. In brief, he only gave way to his enemies over those points on which the opposition was united. The princes had little interest in investiture, and he was therefore able to refuse concessions on this point to the pope. The pope had no desire to stand in his way, if he was truly repentant, and could not refuse him absolution if he sought it before the meeting at Augsburg took place. This precisely is what happened. Immediately after the Diet of Tribur, he sent an embassy to Rome to secure his absolution. When this failed, he decided on a more dramatic move and shortly before Christmas, taking the princes by surprise, crossed the Alps and, meeting the pope at Canossa, obtained absolution at the pope's hand and was received back into communion with the Church.

The dramatic scene at Canossa was a real act of personal humiliation, but it saved the cause of the German monarchy. Henry had to agree to accept the pope's judgement in his differences with the German princes; but the insertion of a clause *nisi impedimentum* into the agreement gave him a valid excuse for prevarication. Moreover, although Gregory maintained that Henry still remained suspended from the exercise of his royal rights, it was difficult to argue convincingly that whereas excommunication had deprived him of the right to rule, the raising of the ban did not restore him to the kingship. Finally, the reconciliation between Henry and the Church was a serious disillusionment for the German princes who were intent on deposition, and the breach between them and Gregory, for which Henry had worked since Tribur, was thus consummated. For them, Henry's secret flight to Italy was a deliberate breach of the Tribur agreement, and they forthwith decided to elect another ruler in Henry's place. For this purpose they met at Forchheim on March 13th, 1077, but they were now compelled to act without the pope. Not only did Henry bar the road from Italy, thus preventing the pope from travelling to Germany, but the papal legate who was present at Forch-heim, acting on the pope's instructions, expressly requested them to postpone the election of an anti-king. When the princes elected Rudolf Rheinfelden in 1077, they therefore no longer possessed the same power or standing as at Tribur in the preceding year. Gregory refused to recognize their nominee and attempted to adopt the role of mediator, calling on both parties to grant him safe-conduct and accept his judgement. But the Saxons were bent not on reconciliation, but on Henry's deposition, and Henry, seeing his star in the ascendant, was adamant. Meanwhile, the apparent hesitancy of the papacy, and its constant negotiations with both parties, lowered Gregory's prestige; soon his adherents were openly expressing doubts of his constancy. The great coalition against Henry was visibly disintegrating.

Canossa was thus a political victory for Henry IV. Now that he was again in communion with the Church, the loyalty of the German bishops, who had begun to waver in 1076, was restored. The effects of the excommunication were undone in the eyes of ordinary people. Rudolf of Rheinfelden, on the other hand, was too evidently the nominee of the princes to obtain wide popular support, and in the eyes of the Saxons he was suspect as a Swabian. Particularly significant was the support accorded to Henry by the rising towns, Mainz and Worms in the west, Regensburg, Augsburg and Würzburg in the south and east. The rebels experienced difficulty in keeping the Saxons in the field, for they were not interested in the cause either of the princes or of the papacy. Furthermore, Rudolf's resources were quickly exhausted through the rapacity of his aristocratic supporters, and when as a result he began to lay hands on Church lands he fell into disrepute. When at last in 1080 Gregory gave up hopes of mediation and declared himself for Rudolf, again placing Henry under the ban of the Church, his action misfired. Even Rudolf rebelled against the pope's presumptuous declara-

tion that the new German king was a vassal of the Holy See. The renewed excommunication of Henry, on the other hand, was widely regarded as an act of persecution. In any case, the moment was unhappily chosen, for six months later, in October 1080, Rudolf fell mortally wounded on the field of battle.

Thereafter the civil war in Germany quickly lost every semblance of its original character, and became an open struggle for aggrandizement on the part of the princes. It was not easy to find a new anti-king, but eventually Hermann of Salm, a count from Luxemburg, was elected. He was an insignificant character, *inane portans nomen regis* (as one chronicler wrote), and it is characteristic that Henry felt strong enough to leave him to be dealt with by his adherents, under the leadership of the new royalist Duke of Swabia, Frederick of Hohenstaufen, to whom Henry had given the hand of his daughter, while he himself crossed the Alps to secure the imperial crown and deal the Gregorians a final blow. In Germany, the struggle was practically over. The mass of the people were avidly desirous of peace, and the divisions among his foes enabled Henry to gain the upper hand. Using every means of persuasion, and affirming that he had no wish to displant ancient Saxon privileges, he genuinely sought to reconcile the Saxon peasantry. By 1085, when Hermann was compelled to fly to Denmark for safety, Henry was again in control of almost every bishopric in the kingdom. Even in the ranks of the opposition, Hermann's uselessness was recognized, and a new candidate appeared in the person of Eckbert of Meissen. With the death of the former in 1088 and of the latter in 1090, the opposition collapsed. The Saxons made their peace, and in 1091 the last two leaders of the rebellion, Berthold of Carinthia and Welf of Bavaria, submitted. With the death in 1091 of Abbot William of Hirsau, the protagonist of monastic reform, the last flame of opposition to Henry IV expired in Germany.

All now depended on the situation in Italy. Six years earlier, in 1085, Gregory VII had died in exile, after seeing all his hopes crumble. His declaration in favour of Rudolf in 1080 had immediately been answered by Henry who, at the head of the bishops and metropolitans of Germany and Lombardy, had declared him deposed for his crimes and appointed a new pope, Clement III, in his place. Thus to the schism in the empire was added schism in the Church, and Gregory's position became so precarious that he was compelled to seek reconciliation with the Norman prince, Robert Guiscard, on the latter's terms. His whole position now depended on the military support of the Normans and of Matilda of Tuscany. But on the very day on which the German anti-king, Rudolf, fell in battle, Matilda's troops suffered a decisive reverse at Volta, near Mantua, while Robert Guiscard turned away from Italy, led eastward by the ambition of conquering the eastern empire. Thus the way was opened for Henry, and although the struggle was hard, he finally penetrated into Rome, where Gregory held out in the castle of St. Angelo, and was crowned emperor by Clement III in 1084. At this critical juncture, however, Guiscard came to the rescue with overwhelming forces, and Henry was forced to retreat northwards. The Normans captured and sacked Rome, leaving a third of the city in ashes, and then withdrew southwards. Clement III reoccupied the city, and Gregory, whom the Normans had taken with them, after a few months died in Salerno, an exile and a failure.

These reverses had serious repercussions within the Church, and for three years the reformers faltered. The college of cardinals was sharply divided, and Henry showed some astuteness in emphasizing his desire for peace and his regret for Gregory's misfortunes. But the anti-pope, Clement III, was the stumbling-block, and Henry himself, with his undoubted tendency to overplay his hand, was probably not willing to make real concessions, par-

ticularly as the papacy was under Norman control and therefore scarcely free to come to terms, since Guiscard's policy, which was the decisive factor, was anti-imperial. Thus the most opportune moment for a settlement went by unused, and with the election of Urban II in 1088 the Gregorian party again resumed control. Supported by Matilda and the Normans, Urban's power proved unshakable. For seven years, from 1090 to 1097, Henry vainly waged war in Lombardy; but Matilda could not be subdued. Meanwhile Urban advanced the claims of the papacy, forbidding not only lay investiture but also fealty to laymen on the part of the episcopate; the bishops were henceforth only to be bound by oath to the papacy. The pope's part in the first crusade not only raised his standing in Europe, but placed him at the head of a *militia Christi*, which looked to him as its leader. It was not long before it became clear that the opportunity lost after Gregory's death in 1085 would not be repeated, that Henry had no chance of subduing the papacy, and that the continued struggle with the Church was defeating any hope of final pacification. All three successors of Gregory VII — Victor III (1086–1087), Urban II (1088–1099) and Paschal II (1099–1118) — confirmed and renewed the former's sentence of excommunication, thus casting doubt on the validity of all Henry's acts of government. Already in 1089, when the solidity of Henry's position in Germany had become manifest, the opposition had offered its mediation, if he would throw over the anti-pope; but he was unable to bring himself to the point of compromise, and thus the conviction gradually made itself felt that Henry alone stood between the realm and peace. In these circumstances, opposition arose even within his own family, where it was felt that his obstinacy was compromising the dynasty. Already in 1093, Urban had won over the king's son Conrad, whom Henry had had consecrated as his successor in 1087, and Conrad had gone to Italy, married the daughter of Roger of Sicily, placed himself at the head of a league of Lombard cities and received the Lombard crown, which he retained until his death in 1101. Henry himself, despairing of success in Italy, saw the need for settlement, and immediately on his return to Germany in 1097 summoned a meeting of the princes at Mainz to discuss terms of peace. But the more exalted claims set forth by Urban and maintained by his successor, Paschal II, offered little prospect of settlement, Henry was still unshakably determined to maintain his rights of investiture, for which he had struggled so long. The overture which he made to Rome in 1101 was repulsed, and even his final offer to demonstrate his penance by going on crusade proved unacceptable. Thus the issue with the Church was as far from solution as ever, and so long as discord prevailed, there was little hope of permanent betterment in Germany. Italy, on the other hand, was completely out of control: after Henry withdrew in 1097, and still more after the death of his son, the anti-king Conrad, in 1101, German influence collapsed, and Italy was left, in spite of occasional brief imperial campaigns, to develop in independence on its own lines for the next fifty years.

IV

It was in these circumstances that, in 1104, Henry's second son, who had been crowned king as his father's designated successor in 1099, rose in rebellion. Few acts in German history have been more severely castigated than this betrayal of the father by the son, at the very moment when the former seemed to have introduced a new measure of peace and prosperity in Germany. Contemporaries scornfully described his action as "contrary to nature," and Hermann of Tournai, who saw the letter of expostulation written by Henry IV in his plight to the king of France, said that anyone who read it and remained unmoved could only be described as hard-hearted. It was widely held, perhaps not without reason, that the instigator was the pope, and it is far from certain that the plot would have succeeded, in spite of the unscrupulous chicanery of the insurgents, had Henry IV not died, in the midst of the struggle, at Liège, whither he had withdrawn to prepare resistance. His death, on August 7th, 1106, left his rebellious son, Henry V, unchallenged master of the field.

The full story of Henry V's rebellion will never be known, and there is no sure means of deciding what part personal ambition played in his plans. But it is certain that there were substantial heads of disagreement between him and his father, and it seems likely that he was convinced that Henry IV's obduracy was mistaken and ultimately disastrous. Perhaps he realized that a continuation of the struggle with the Church would only undermine still further the power of the crown, and that, if the discord continued, the old emperor would bequeath to his heir, not a stable royal power, but weak and unsubstantiated claims. Probably, also, Henry IV's policy of increasing reliance on and cooperation with the rising towns, and even with the peasantry, was too revolutionary for his son, particularly as royal support of the towns was alienating the German bishops who saw their control of the episcopal cities thereby menaced. In contrast to his father, therefore, Henry V determined to come to terms with the aristocracy, intending thereby to secure the backing of a united Germany for the struggle with the papacy. In the long run his ultimate objects may have been little different from his father's; but there was a radical difference in his methods, which was the result of time and events. If, in 1076, Henry IV had perceived that his best prospect lay in reconciliation with the Church — hence Canossa — by 1105 it was apparent that the persistent discord with the Church was the main source of unrest. Hence, where Henry IV had fought above all to prevent the disruption of the work of the Salian monarchy by the princes, Henry V, when he broke away from his father, deliberately acknowledged the aristocratic character of the German constitution. "The removal of a single person," he is reported to have said, shortly after the beginning of his revolt, "even if he is the supreme head of the State, is a reparable injury to the realm; but the destruction of the princes is the destruction of the very kingdom." In these words he implicitly designated himself the representative of the princes, and in this respect the successor of the anti-kings, Rudolf of Rheinfelden and Hermann of Salm; and although he had, as legitimate heir of the royal dynasty, an independent power which neither Rudolf nor Hermann had ever possessed, the decline in the position of the monarchy was manifest. Henry V had not only to throw over the Salian programme, which had originally provoked the opposition of the nobility to the crown and had created in Germany a party willing to ally with the papacy; he had also, ruling in cooperation with the princes, to accept and sanction the powers and privileges which the aristocracy had usurped during the thirty years in which Henry IV's energies had been diverted by the struggle with the Church. There was some tactical skill in winning the support of the aristocracy so as to oppose a united Germany to the claims of the papacy; but the longer such a policy was pursued the more difficult it became to shake off the control of the aristocracy; and there lay the real test.

Nevertheless, the short-term benefits of the change of ruler were immediately apparent, and within a few months of his father's death Henry V was able to take up the question of investiture with the full support and backing of the German bishops and princes. In face of the papacy Germany was at long last united. But negotiations were not easy, since the pope clung to the extreme demands he had formulated in 1102, and the moderate proposals put forward by Henry in 1107, in which — adopting the compromise views recently sponsored in France and England — he claimed only to confer the indisputably secular *regalia*, were rejected, although (as has been pointed out) these proposals would have satisfied earlier popes, including Gregory VII. A further embassy, dispatched by Henry in 1109, received only the noncommittal answer that the pope claimed only what was canonical and had no intention of diminishing the king's rights. In these circumstances, with the full support of Germany, Henry set out for Italy at the head of an army of 30,000 men, intent on restoring imperial rights and securing a final settlement with the papacy. Matilda of Tuscany, long the mainstay of the papal party, submitted to Henry, whom she made her heir, thus cancelling her earlier gift of her lands to the Holy See. Paschal realized that a decision could no longer be postponed and — still determined to avoid all forms of lay investiture — made the proposal which Henry accepted, that, in return for a renunciation of the royal right of investiture, the churches should restore to the crown all *regalia* and appurtenant lands acquired since the reign of Charles the Great. But when the pope published the treaty, which Henry had already confirmed, a tumult arose among both the prelates, who feared the loss of their fiefs, and the German nobility, who foresaw the loss of the fiefs they held from the churches. Paschal was compelled to denounce the agreement, which he was impotent to enforce, and was left to face the king, who took him and the cardinals prisoner and — using the threat of schism — compelled Paschal to issue a privilege, granting him rights of investiture. Once again all Henry demanded was recognition of his right to confer *regalia*, which would have been accepted without difficulty by reformers in the days of Gregory VII and Urban II; but now a storm arose, the pope's action was condemned at a council in Vienne, and Paschal was faced by the threat of revolt among the French bishops. At a synod in Rome in March 1112 he was forced to retrace his steps, and in 1116 he finally issued an express revocation of his privilege.

These events had little effect on Henry V's position in Germany. The council of Vienne held him up to the obloquy of Christendom, but although the Archbishop of Vienne pressed for excommunication, he failed to secure papal assent, which alone would have given the sentence wide-reaching effect. As a result of cutting away from Henry IV's policy, the crown was evidently still too strong to fear a repetition of the events of 1076. But although the Church was no longer able to sow discord in Germany, the inherent weaknesses in Henry's position, due to his close dependence on the princes, now began to make themselves apparent. Despite his ruthlessness and energy, he was never able to restore peace in Germany or repress the plundering of feudal marauders. Nor was he able to rehabilitate the crown lands, which had been wasted and pillaged during the civil wars, until nothing but scattered fragments remained. He was not slow in recognizing the necessity for a revival of the efficient administration which had been the mark of the earlier period of Henry IV's government, and was credited with the intention of instituting an inquest on the model of the English Domesday Survey, and on this basis of introducing a system of royal taxation. But these projects came to nothing; the opposition was too strong, and unlike his father Henry had neither the strong convictions nor the power to resist it. It was the same when he attempted, in 1112, to resume vacant fiefs in Saxony for the crown: this brought him face to face with the rising Supplinburg and Ascanian dynasties, while an attempt to reassert his rights in Frisia raised rebellion in the northwest of the kingdom. By the end of 1114 Saxony was in full revolt, and early in 1115 the Saxon leader, Lothar of Supplinburg, won a decisive victory at the battle of Welfesholz. Henry was still confident enough to leave German affairs in the hands of his nephews, Conrad and Frederick of Staufen, and himself

go to Italy in order to secure possession of the lands of Matilda of Tuscany, who had died in 1115; but unrest continued during his absence and after his return. After the battle of Welfesholz, the sentence of excommunication proclaimed three years earlier at the synod of Vienne was promulgated in Germany. For a time it looked as though a junction of the feudal and reforming opposition would be effected, bringing with it a return to the evil conditions of Henry IV's reign.

In these circumstances Henry redoubled his efforts to come to terms with the Church, but for many months without positive results. The pope, fearing a repetition of the violent measures of 1111, refused a conference, and when Henry appeared in Italy in 1116, fled to a safe refuge with the Normans. Paschal II's death in 1118, far from bringing about improved relations, resulted in a deterioration, for Henry, having failed in an attempt to lay hands on the new pontiff, Gelasius II, set up an antipope, and was promptly excommunicated; while Gelasius sought refuge first in southern Italy and then in France, where he died in 1119. He was succeeded by the Archbishop of Vienne who had first excommunicated Henry in 1112, and whose first act as pope, under the title Calixtus II, was to renew the excommunication. But an attempt, in a synod at Rheims in 1119 to renew the unqualified condemnation of lay investiture, failed in face of opposition from both clergy and laity, and Calixtus was forced to the realization that some form of compromise was unavoidable. Henry also, by now fully conscious of the measure of his peril, was ready to make his peace with both princes and pope. The papal sentence of excommunication had been proclaimed by legates at synods at Cologne and Fritzlar in May 1119, and there were rumours of an imminent meeting of the princes with the intention of deposing the king. This threat, recalling with all vividness the evil days of 1076, was decisive and Henry placed himself without reserve in the hands of the princes, promising to obey their decisions in matters both of Church and of State. In Germany he gave orders for each and every individual to be restored to his "rights" and properties, and in return he received an assurance from the princes that, in the settlement with the Church, they would firmly maintain the honour of the emperor.

Thus the settlement between Church and State, when it came about, was the work of the princes, standing like a third power in an independent position between king and pope. A commission of twelve princes, chosen equally from both parties, was appointed to prepare the terms of settlement, and at the council of Würzburg in 1121 Henry had to agree to set aside his own wishes and abide by their decision. The princes, observing their earlier promise, gave solid support to the emperor's claims in the negotiations which now began with the Holy See; but the whole course of proceedings is evidence of the distance affairs in Germany had travelled since the beginning of Henry IV's reign. The princes, deciding high policy, were now manifestly the masters. Nevertheless, the evident unity of sentiment within Germany was impressive, and doubtless contributed towards producing a conciliatory attitude in Rome. Calixtus sent word to Henry that his intention was not to diminish but to enhance the honour of the empire, and a further council was held at Worms, at which, on September 23rd, 1122, agreement was reached. Henry agreed to renounce the traditional investiture with ring and staff — a form of investiture which through age-old tradition implied conferment of the ecclesiastical office — but in exchange the pope recognized his right to confer the *regalia* by investiture with the ·sceptre. This latter investiture was to take place before consecration, thus ensuring that the elected prelate should not enter into his duties until he had sworn homage and fealty to the king. In addition, Henry obtained the valuable concession that elections in Germany should be carried out in his presence, thus en-

abling him to bring due influence to bear. Royal control over the German church was, therefore, substantially maintained. In Italy and Burgundy, on the contrary, Henry's concessions were more far-reaching. Here no form of election in the king's presence was granted, and the king agreed that the bishops should be consecrated (thus receiving full administrative control over their dioceses) before the grant of *regalia*, which were to be conferred within six months of consecration. This difference reflected the decline of royal power in Italy, where the civil wars had already *de facto* deprived the king of control over the Lombard episcopacy. Even so, it is surprising that Henry was willing to grant formal recognition to this revolutionary change; but the explanation was in all probability his acquisition, in 1116, of the Mataldine lands, which provided an alternative foundation for royal power in Italy. Here, if properly used, was a basis for royal power far more stable and assured than the doubtful loyalty of the Lombard bishops, whose position as instruments of the monarchy was assailed not only by the currents of ecclesiastical reform but also by the rise of the communes, which were already disputing episcopal control of the Lombard cities.

The Concordat of Worms was no final settlement of the conflict of Church and State; for no formal agreement could dispose of the insoluble problems arising from the two-fold loyalties of the bishops and prelates. Moreover, the papal concessions, which were admittedly far-reaching, were hotly criticized by reforming circles when the agreement was published at the Lateran Council in 1123, and were only accepted after it had been pointed out that there was no question of approving the disputed points, but only of tolerating them for the sake of peace. It was, furthermore, a fact that, whereas Henry V's concessions were granted to the Church in perpetuity, Calixtus' charter was addressed to Henry V alone; and whatever the reasons for this divergence may have been, there is no doubt that it enabled the Church to maintain that the concession of election in the king's presence — which was the main source of contention — was only a personal concession to Henry, which did not extend to his successors. Already as early as 1125, at the election of Henry V's successor, Lothar II, this view emerged as a serious political argument. Nevertheless these facts should not blind us to the importance of the Concordat of 1122, which — as contemporaries were well aware — did at long last introduce an atmosphere of peace and concord. After fifty years of struggle, emperor and pope had at length discovered a practical *modus vivendi*. Although many points were held over for the future, a breathing-space had been secured in which to review and repair the damage of half-a-century of civil strife. The world-shaking issues over which Gregory VII and Henry IV had fought intransigently were for the moment appeased. But the cost in Germany and throughout the empire was immense. The power of the monarchy had been shaken to its foundations. Peace had been restored between *regnum* and *sacerdotium*; but to restore peace and order and government in Germany was another question. Here, in spite of Henry IV's life-long struggle for his inheritance, the old order had passed beyond recall. In the welter of war and rapine and confusion, Germany had passed over into a new age; it had undergone a revolution, which left its marks for all time on German history.

THE GREGORIAN REFORM

CATHERINE F. BOYD

Miss Boyd, professor of mediaeval history at Carleton College, Minnesota, since 1953, received her undergraduate training at Radcliffe College and her graduate training at Harvard University where she took her doctorate (1934) under two distinguished historians, Gaetano Salvemini and George La Piana. Over a long period of years, Professor Boyd examined the records of diocese after diocese throughout northern and central Italy to learn precisely and authoritatively the constitution of the mediaeval churches of Italy as well as the economic basis of its life. This selection from her *Tithes and Parishes in Medieval Italy* illuminates the accomplishments of the Gregorian movement at one level and its failures at another. Her work provides an antidote to some of the generalizations made in other selections by demonstrating clearly the economic stake contested by the ecclesiastical and lay magnates of the eleventh century.

THE conditions which had originated in the Italian parishes in the tenth century continued unchanged into the eleventh century, when their disastrous effects upon religious life became clearly visible. The monk Donizo, in his versified life of Matilda of Tuscany, tells how the Tuscan bishops sold parish churches to both laymen and priests, to the demoralization of the people. The history of some of these churches can be traced through the century. In 1009 the parish church of Creti in Arezzo was bestowed by the bishop as a prebend upon the archdeacon of his cathedral, with the right of unrestricted alienation; the archdeacon might assign or bequeath the church to another priest or give it as a benefice to a layman, provided the stipulated rent was paid to the bishop. Two generations later the church had become the benefice of a group of nine *milites*. Now practically in ruins, it was retroceded to the bishopric by the knights, who promised to refrain in the future from violence within the church precincts. Of the tithes of the parish, they restored only a fourth, presumably retaining the rest in their possession.

Numerous other examples illustrate the way in which parish churches and their tithes had come to be regarded as objects of proprietary right, to be exploited by clergy and laymen alike. In Lucca, where the concessions in *livello* were in this period being transformed into fiefs, the charges imposed by the bishops upon the parish priests also assumed a more feudal character. One parish was let by Bishop Grimizzo to a priest in return for a money rent and a horse if needed for service in the imperial host. Bishop Anselm I, though he favored ecclesiastical reform, confirmed the grants of parishes to laymen which had been made by his predecessors. In the regions farther north the same practices obtained. Bishops helped themselves to the tithes of their parish churches or shared them with their vassals for political purposes. Marquis Boniface of Tuscany at one time held thirteen parish churches from the bishop of Reggio, who shared the revenues of fourteen others with the local

Reprinted by permission from *Tithes and Parishes in Medieval Italy* by Catherine F. Boyd (Cornell University Press, 1952).

knights. In the Piedmontese bishoprics numerous churches and tithes were held by laymen, although here, to a greater extent than elsewhere in Italy, the tithe was annexed to manorial churches without parochial rights. Ulric-Manfred, count of Turin, and his daughter Adelaide had in their possession many churches and their revenues. When a reformer in the eleventh century used the term "simony," he had before his eyes this whole complex of mercenary transactions which resulted from the growth of the proprietary system of churches and the extension of the proprietary idea to the parishes. It will be noted that the clergy as well as the laity exercised proprietary rights over the lower churches, treating them as if they were their private property and disposing of their revenues as if they were private income.

Abuses of a moral order were undoubtedly fostered by these practices. Clerical marriage was of course widespread in Italy, as well as less legitimate relations. Rathier of Verona, late in the tenth century, stated that if he tried to enforce clerical celibacy in his diocese, he would be left without a clergy. In Milan the clergy married according to the forms of civil law and claimed that marriage was a custom permitted to the church of St. Ambrose. Clerical marriage became doubly dangerous to ecclesiastical order when combined with the leasing of churches to the clergy under tenurial forms which gave them complete control of church property; there was a real possibility that church offices and property might become hereditary.

That the first generation of reformers in the eleventh century was disturbed about conditions in the Italian rural parishes is evident from the writings of the two most influential among them — Peter Damiani and Humbert of Moyenmoutier. Both prelates denounced the widespread traffic in parishes and tithes, and abuse for which they held the episcopate chiefly responsible.

There are bishops [writes Damiani] who hand over parish churches to laymen; such prelates sin the more grievously in that they are committing the sacrilege of profaning sacred things; and to those whom they seem to benefit they dispense a mortal poison. For to divert tithes to laymen, is not this to give them a poison of which they will die? Add further that just cause is given to the parishioners of such churches for withdrawing their obedience from their mother churches and not paying them their due tribute of tithes.

Damiani paints a highly colored picture of the Italian bishops of his time, surrounded by armed vassals whom they reward for their services by concessions of church property. The typical bishop is attended, not as he should be by the divers orders of the clergy, but by shield-bearers and lancers. When he has given away all the lands of his see, then he has recourse to parish churches and tithes as benefices for laymen. This dishonest liberality deprives the poor of their patrimony and discourages the parishioners of such churches from paying their tithes. While reserving his fiercest invectives for the bishops, Damiani does not spare the lay aristocracy which was benefiting from these abuses, castigating especially the unseemly zeal with which they seek to transform temporary grants of church property into hereditary tenures.

What shall I say of the sale of church property? For not only properties which are leased by a contract of enfiteusi or originate in such a right, and those which are granted libellario nomine, but even those which laymen receive under the mere name of benefice cannot henceforth be revoked or restored to the churches. The hands of the robbers are so smeared with the glue of devilish tenacity that once they have acquired property in any way they refuse to surrender it to the church; and not only hold it themselves by proprietary right during their lifetime but also transmit it to their offspring. Laymen beg you for ecclesiastical property, force their importunities upon you, urge you with entreaties to give them this property, not to be recorded in a formal contract, but merely as a benefice; which, however, once granted, is just the same as if it had been inscribed on bronze tablets with a steel pen.

Damiani makes it clear that the taint of the simoniacal heresy rests upon the mercenary transactions that are taking place in the rural parishes and that the priest who pays for a rural parish (*plebs agrorum*) is guilty of simony no less than those who traffic in the greater churches.

Cardinal Humbert seems to have shared the contemporary German prejudice against the Italian church as a sink of iniquity and the Italian episcopate as peculiarly corrupt.

Alas! I remember how often I have seen [in Italy] the pavements of noble basilicas ploughed up and pigs and cattle stabled within their walls. And for these atrocities, not the Vandal, Goth, or Hun is responsible, not the Lombard or the Hungarian, but the simoniac. The tithes, too, and the oblations the simoniac sells or gives to laymen in diabolical contracts. Leases of church property flow into lay hands, together with charters and documents bearing the signatures of these simoniacs, so that the ancient rights and canonical privileges of God's churches are conceded to laymen forever.

Since the reformers diagnosed so correctly the conditions in the Italian parishes, it is pertinent at this point to inquire into the place of the lower churches, both baptismal churches and those of a lesser order, in the program of reform that was set forth in 1059.

*   *   *

In April 1059 the Easter synod assembled at the Lateran. During the previous decade the papacy had been purified and regenerated through the action of the lay power, the pious emperor Henry III, the most distinguished member of the Salian dynasty. One of Henry's appointees, Leo IX, had launched the papal reforming movement in a series of synods, mostly in France and Germany, which had condemned simony and clerical marriage. By 1059 the reforming movement was well under way. But political conditions had radically changed. Henry III, sympathetic towards attempts to reform clerical morals, had died three years before, and the new German king, Henry IV, was a minor. Godfrey of Lorraine, a former rebel against the Empire and now as husband of Beatrice of Tuscany in control of the large Canossan domains in central Italy, supported the reformers. The reigning pope, Nicholas II, also from Lorraine and bishop of Florence before his elevation to the papacy, was Godfrey's protégé. The revolutionary Pataria, led by the deacon Ariald and the noble Landulf, was agitating for "free elections" of the archbishops of Milan and attacking the married clergy in that city. Milan in 1059 was the seat of a veritable civil war. The Pataria was in open rebellion against the imperialist archbishop, and Ariald was already negotiating for an alliance with the papacy. This alliance was consummated late in the year.

Against the background of these events 113 bishops met in the Lateran basilica, their deliberations guided by a brilliant constellation of ecclesiastical statesmen: Nicholas II; Boniface, cardinal of Sant'-Albano, his close adviser, first to sign after the Pope himself the electoral decree which liberated the papacy from the control of Roman noble factions; Peter Damiani, recently raised to the cardinalate against his will, the epitome of the Italian monastic spirit; Hildebrand, the future Gregory VII, not yet archdeacon of the Roman Church, an Italian but not of the episcopal aristocracy and perhaps partly for that reason more accessible to new ideas; and Humbert of Moyenmoutier, a native of Lorraine and still a comparatively young man, who had come to Rome as secretary of Leo IX and had steadily risen to influence in the papal curia. Humbert a year before, in his *Three Books Against the Simoniacs,* had launched "the first frontal attack against the whole position of laymen within the Church," which was soon to give a new direction to the program of reform.

Three of the decrees passed by the Lateran synod of 1059 are relevant to our purpose. Canon 3 discloses the organization of the secular clergy which the reformers proposed to substitute wherever possible for the abuses of their time. After renewing Leo IX's decree against the marriage of priests, deacons, and subdeacons, and forbidding married priests to celebrate mass (canon 2), the council prescribed that the clergy of those orders (i.e., priests, deacons, and subdeacons) who in obedience to the reforming decrees had preserved their chastity, should henceforth sleep and eat together near their churches, hold in common the revenues of those churches, and strive earnestly to realize the apostolic life, namely the common life. Fliche thus comments: "Nicholas II proposes that the common life shall be adopted by the universal church. . . . An attempt is made to prevent the abuse of clerical marriage by making illicit relations more difficult, by organizing mutual surveillance, and by preventing the clergy from amassing private fortunes." This comment stresses somewhat too much the negative and disciplinary aspect of the canonical movement which is here unveiled. The resurrection of the life of the apostolic Church on which it was based was the leitmotiv of the Italian reformers in the eleventh century and was rooted in a tradition of the common life of the clergy which, although almost obliterated in the darker periods, had never been entirely extinguished. The Carolingian rulers had fostered the idea of the canonical life of the clergy, and reforming bishops of the ninth century had had a temporary success in introducing this life into their cathedrals. Occasionally canonries were founded in rural parishes, for it would seem that the ideal behind the Carolingian legislation was to extend the reform to at least the larger baptismal churches which had a numerous clergy.

At the beginning of the eleventh century the canonical life was revived in Italy under the sponsorship of eremitical monasticism and evidently was introduced into some of the rural parish churches even earlier than into the cathedrals. Thus in 1005 at Val de Castro, St. Romuald persuaded the local clergy to abandon simony and, instead of living after the manner of laymen, to obey a prior and live in a community. From a monastic milieu the idea spread to reforming bishops and sympathetic laymen. The canonical life was established in a rural parish of Asti in 1024, in Lucca in 1025, where fourteen canons, at the invitation of Bishop John II, united in the common life in the rural baptistery of Santa Maria a Monte. In 1056 some pious laymen gave half of a rural church, evidently a private church and not a parish, to three priests, on condition that they should pursue the common life therein, "dwelling in chastity in houses close to the church." In Milan, Ariald received by gift a private church, within which he organized a semimonastic community, where the clergy lived from a common purse, ate at a common board while listening to sacred readings, celebrated the offices seven times a day, and dedicated themselves to a life of individual poverty in imitation of the apostolic community. This church had an irresistible appeal not only for the townspeople but for others who flocked in from the outlying castles and villages, glad to have a church "where they could hear God's word with free minds and partake of the sacraments." In 1058, just before his election to the papacy, Nicholas II, then Bishop Gerard of Florence, had introduced the canonical life into several Florentine parish churches. There is evidence, too, that under the influence of the reforming popes of the 1050's, the Roman clergy also were adopting the common life. Hildebrand is known to have sympathized with the movement and at a later time, as Pope Gregory VII, composed a rule for the canons of such churches.

The most enthusiastic advocate of the movement in Italy, however, was Cardinal Damiani, who devoted to it several of his most eloquent letters. He did not intend to force this life upon all the secular clergy; he states clearly that is only for canons, i.e., the clergy of cathedrals and collegiate churches. But it is evident that he regarded it as the only life possible for a true cleric and desired it to be held up as an ideal for all the secular clergy. Moreover, given the collegiate structure of the Italian rural parish, composed of a central baptistery with its cluster of subordinate chapels, it is permissible to believe that Damiani, writing with Italian conditions before his eyes, wanted the common life of the clergy to be fostered in the rural parishes as a weapon against simony, as well as in resurrection of a traditional ideal. In any case, there is ample evidence in the documents that this was the goal of the leading Italian reformers of this period. The canonical movement, incorporated into the papal program in 1059, remained a vital element in the reform movement in Italy to the end of the eleventh century.

*　　*　　*

Attractive and inspiring as the canonical reform was as a vehicle for the moral regeneration of the clergy, there were some members of the synod of 1059 who realized that it was not an adequate solution for the ills besetting the Church. Already there were in the Roman curia men who were convinced that the evil lay chiefly not in the corruption of the clergy but in lay control of churches and their revenues. Of this group Humbert had already made himself the spokesman, if indeed he had not created the group, by his *Adversus Simoniacos*. His uncompromising hostility to lay control of the Church was voiced in the sixth canon passed by the synod: "No cleric or priest shall receive a church from a laymen, either gratis or for a price." Nothing is said here about lay investiture, which was after all a technicality, nor is the prohibition restricted to bishoprics and abbacies. The decree lays the ax at the root of the whole system of lay proprietary rights, whether exercised by the emperor in appointing an archbishop of Milan or by a knight in appointing a parish priest. However, having enunciated this drastic principle, the Church moved very slowly in enforcing it during the next nineteen years, and it is interesting to speculate as to the

reasons why. Humbert died in 1061, having previously refused election to the papacy. Nicholas' successor, Alexander II, while a sincere reformer, seems to have been of a temporizing character, inclined to compromise with the lay aristocracy and with the imperial government. He was the former Anselmo da Baggio, member of a family of *capitanei* which held concessions of parishes and tithes in the Milanese contado. He was one of four candidates for the office of archbishop of Milan in 1045 who were rejected by the Emperor, and was the chief organizer of the Pataria. As bishop of Lucca from 1057 to 1073 he was a zealous promoter of the canonical reform, but local documents still in the episcopal archives of Lucca show that in his relations with the lay feudality he followed in the footsteps of his predecessors. He continued to be bishop of Lucca after becoming Pope in 1061, and we are presented with the curious spectacle of a pope renewing and confirming the "diabolical contracts" denounced by Humbert in his *Adversus Simoniacos*. He made his position clear, however, in a letter which he addressed as Pope to the cathedral chapter of Lucca. For a long time, he wrote, the evil of simony had desolated the church of Lucca; no cleric, however religious, educated, or honest he might be, could obtain an ecclesiastical office without the aid of money; on the other hand, if a cleric had the necessary means he could purchase his ordination as priest without passing through minor orders as required by canon law; the church and its property in Lucca were sold by vile traffickers like any earthly object. After condemning simony, the bull then forbade further concessions of church lands to laymen other than leaseholds to peasants and small cultivators. Excepted from the prohibition, however, was property already let out as benefices to laymen. This limiting clause was indicative of the policy which the Church was almost forced to take, and marked out the path in which even the reformers walked for the next few generations. Needing the support of the lay aristocracy in the removal of the most crying abuses, the Church could not afford to estrange them from the cause of moral reform by attacking too vigorously their vested interests in church property.

The most urgent single question in Alexander's pontificate was undoubtedly the affair of Milan, where his election to the papacy had thrown fuel on the flames and confirmed the Lombard bishops in their support of an imperialist antipope, Cadalus of Parma. Alexander, on his side, allied himself with the increasingly radical Pataria and appointed the Milanese noble Herlembald the military leader of the movement in Lombardy. The Pataria is too complex to be analyzed here. A more recent interpretation of this perplexing movement is that it was not a class struggle, an uprising of the depressed classes, but a party struggle in which all classes mingled on one side or the other and in which the major issues were canonical elections and clerical marriage. This primarily religious movement took on a revolutionary guise because necessarily directed against the ruling classes, the Lombard episcopate and the high feudatories, identified with the Lombard *Reichskirche*. In the crises of the movement its chief support came from the poorer classes, the artisans and petty bourgeoisie, but its leaders were nobles and it seems to have been connected in some obscure way with the discontent of the lower nobility. At any rate, with civil war raging in Lombardy and the Lombard episcopate ranged on the side of an antipope, the papacy was scarcely in a position to launch a full-scale attack on lay proprietorship of churches and their property.

Whatever the reasons may be, the Lateran synods until 1078 showed a certain reserve on the subject of the lower churches and their revenues. Canon 6 of the synod of 1059 had not explicitly condemned the holding of churches by laymen, although this principle certainly seems to be implied. In regard to the tithes, the council had merely ordained

that they must be paid by the laity to the churches and should be at the disposal of the bishops to be distributed by them according to the laws of the Church. Any right to the tithes on the part of the parish churches and their clergy is not mentioned, and there is no prohibition of lay ownership of tithes.

This reticence on the part of the Roman councils is in contrast to the French synods of the eleventh century, which from 1031 on fought to improve the condition of the lower churches. While refraining for a long time from an express condemnation of lay proprietorship of churches, these French councils asserted vigorously and repeatedly the rights of the bishops to spiritual jurisdiction over the priests of private churches and insisted upon the right of the local church to at least a third of its tithes and oblations. The council of Toulouse in 1056 insisted that in proprietary churches a third of the tithes should go to the priest of the church to be administered by him for the benefit of the church under the supervision of the bishop. The synod of Tours in 1060 threatened with excommunication any layman who possessed, sold, or infeudated the oblations or the third of the tithes. Similar provisions were passed by the council of Lillebonne (1080) and two councils of Rouen (1074, 1096). This legislation succeeded in establishing in France the right of the *curé* of an impropriated church to at least a third of the tithes, his *portio congrua*, as it was called at a later period. Since some of the French councils of the eleventh century were presided over by papal legates, we may conclude that this practice was approved by the papacy and constituted part of the papal program of reform.

Not until 1078, however, was the papal policy in regard to lay proprietorship of churches finally clarified. Gregory VII had in 1075 issued the decree against lay investiture which brought to a head the long pending struggle between papacy and Empire. Provoked by Henry IV's appointment of an archbishop of Milan, it may be regarded as the assumption by Gregory of the Humbertine attitude of uncompromising hostility towards lay control of church property and personnel, which had been in abeyance during the long pontificate of Alexander II. The investiture decree of 1075 is known to us only through a brief mention by the Milanese chronicler Arnulf, who simply says that the Pope forbade the king henceforth to have any rights in bestowing bishoprics and removed all secular persons from investitures of churches. The decrees of the Lateran synod of November 1078 appear in full in Gregory's *Register*. They threaten with excommunication any knight or lay person who does not surrender to the Church ecclesiastical lands which he has either usurped or received from unworthy priests without the consent of the bishops or abbots. They condemn investitures of churches by emperor, king, or any lay person, whether man or woman. With regard to the tithes, the council took the drastic step of condemning lay possession of tithes even when they had been conceded by the episcopate. The bishops present at the synod were commanded to notify the laity that they were committing sacrilege and endangering their souls' salvation unless they yielded their tithes to the Church. Thus was proclaimed in full the Gregorian program as regards lay proprietorship of churches and tithes. It is noteworthy that this legislation applied to all churches, both upper and lower. It was confirmed in this respect by the March synod of 1080, which, while stressing bishoprics and abbacies, stated that the decrees applied to the lower churches as well. "We ordain similarly concerning the lower ecclesiastical dignities" (canon 1).

In view of the bitter realities facing the reformers, most of the bishops present must have realized the utter impossibility of enforcing these decrees. In fact, it may even be questioned whether the decrees were intended to be more than a statement of principle, to be enforced by reforming bishops and local synods whenever possible. The limits on possibility are illustrated by a decree of the French synod of Gerona in 1078, the first French synod actually to condemn lay ownership of churches. Canon 13 declares: "We know that churches do not pertain to laymen; but where they cannot be taken away from them, we at least forbid laymen absolutely to possess their oblations and firstfruits." Remembering that the reform movement found a relatively sympathetic reception in France, this decree permits us to gauge the resistance met by the reformers when they attacked the lay proprietary system. The synod admits the impossibility of recovering all the churches from laymen; it condemns the principle of lay ownership, at the same time making it clear that the practice will be tolerated.

In 1895, in an essay on the *Eigenkirche* which has become classic, Ulrich Stutz maintained that in 1059 the decision was taken at Rome to concentrate upon the struggle to free the bishops and abbacies from lay control and to postpone the struggle for the lower churches in order not to alienate the lay aristocracy together with royalty. This thesis contains a large element of truth. But it requires to be qualified slightly in the light of our fuller knowledge. It ignores the activity of the French synods after 1059, of which Stutz seems to have been unaware. It does not give full weight to the Roman legislation of 1078 and 1080. And it does not take into account a fact unknown to Stutz, because hidden in local Italian documents, that in the eleventh century and largely as a result of the activities of the reformers, the parish churches of Italy established their legal right to a share in the tithes, a process analogous to that which happened in France but evidently without the aid of synodal legislation.

There is a considerable body of evidence in existence, both from the eleventh century and later, to prove that the Gregorian reformers in their writings and in their practices as bishops of Italian dioceses, claimed for the parish churches a fourth of the tithes, the so-called *quartese,* leaving the remainder at the disposal of the bishops. Since the tithe had been instituted by the Carolingian rulers of Italy to provide the parish churches with an income and since, even during the period when the parishes were being dispossessed of their tithes by the lay aristocracy, their legal title to the tithes had not been questioned, both the theory and the practice of the Gregorian reformers present themselves as strange anomalies, aberrations from canon law. Why did the reformers not demand all the tithes for the parish churches? An answer to this question entails an exploration of local documents showing the appearance of the *quartese* in Italian practice and an examination of the writings of the Roman canonists of the Gregorian period.

* * *

Early in the eleventh century there seems to have developed in northern Italy the practice of reserving to the parish church a share in the tithes normally fixed at a fourth. The earliest implied recognition of the right of the parish churches to this fourth occurs in a charter of 1032 in which the bishop of Parma gives as a benefice to a canon of his cathedral the parish church of Malandriano together with a fourth of the tithes, promising that when the remaining three-fourths are restored by the knights who have usurped them, they will also form part of the benefice. This seems to indicate that the church was already in possession of the fourth, presumably reserved to it by previous bishops and evidently respected by the *milites* who held the rest of the tithes. Another example, also without the use of the word *quartesium,* comes from Padua, where in 1045 the bishop impropriated three-fourths of the parish tithes of Pernumia to his cathedral chapter, reserving a fourth to the parish church itself. Evidently the custom prevailed, in both lay and ecclesiastical impropriations, of reserving a fourth of the tithes for the exclusive use of the church in whose parish they were gathered. A Placentine document of 1038 varies a little; in receiving from Marquis Hugh, "of the race of the Lombards" (i.e., a local feudatory), a donation of two-thirds of the tithes of Port'Albera to the cathedral chapter, the bishop of Piacenza reserves a third of the tithes of Port'Albera to the local church. The first authentic use of the word *quartese* comes to light in a Paduan document of 1076, in which the bishop of Padua bestows upon a monastery "the entire product of the tithe called *quartese* from the villa of Macerata." This grant of the *quartese* to a monastery was an obvious violation of the custom which seems to have been forming for the protection of the parish churches. Similar violations may have helped to provoke the action of sixteen parish priests in the following year when they appealed to the Emperor's delegates to protect them in their persons and property and especially in possession of their *quartesi.* Anyone familiar with early canon law will immediately recognize in this parochial fourth, as in the French third of the same period, the survival of ancient canonical procedure. The law of quadripartition had evidently survived in this form, with the important modification that the *quartese,* the lineal descendant of the fourth of the clergy, has become the portion of the parish church itself.

The parochial fourth became generalized throughout northern Italy in the course of the eleventh century. In the South, the Normans introduced the threefold division of the tithes which prevailed in France, one third to the local church, the rest under the administration of the bishop. It is of course impossible to fix the precise moment at which these practices originated. In the light of the numerous Lucchese documents of the tenth century which show that concessions of tithes and parishes to laymen were always in multiples of a fourth, it seems a not unreasonable suggestion that the parochial fourth may have originated in that century to assure the parish churches at least a minimum revenue. But this is sheer conjecture. If such a rule did exist at this early period it was frequently violated; for in many cases the entire parish and its revenues were ceded to the knights.

The universality of this practice of reserving either a fourth or a third of the tithe to the parish churches in the eleventh century leads one to believe that it had a legal basis, which can only have been ancient canon law. The early dates of some of the documents mentioning this practice show that it preceded the papal reforming movement. But it was certainly accepted and propagated by the Gregorians as part of the restoration of canon law which they were promoting. Before the Gregorian Reform there was a great deal of uncertainty as to what the law of the Church really was. Collections of canons circulated widely but were permeated with conflicting influences. At the beginning of the eleventh century there was a marked revival of interest in canon law, as manifested in such collections as that of Burchard of Worms. In 1051 this revival took a new direction when Humbert, in compiling his *Sentences*, "the first manual of the reforming movement," adopted as his criterion for the selection of canons the tradition of the Roman Church. Subsequently a group of reformers in the entourage of Gregory VII pursued, with the encouragement of the Pope, an investigation into early church law and compiled collections of canons. In assembling their texts, the Gregorian canonists accepted unquestioningly only laws which had emanated from or been approved by the Holy See, excluding so far as possible Germanic, Celtic, Frankish, and episcopal law. In this respect the Roman canonical collections of the Gregorian period stand in marked contrast to earlier collections, such as that of Burchard of Worms, which had been much more eclectic in their standards.

The law of the Roman Church before the intrusion of Germanic, Celtic, and feudal influences had laid great stress upon the unity of the diocese and upon episcopal jurisdiction over all the churches, clergy, and church property within it. Roman legislation of the Gregorian period increasingly bears the imprint of these conceptions, and the unity of the diocese, broken both by the growth of the lay proprietary system and by the development of monastic exemptions, became the guiding principle in the administrative reorganization of the Church. Moreover, in the ancient canons the reformers rediscovered the law of quadripartite division of church revenues which had been formulated in the period of the unitary patrimony, and this they applied to the tithes. The most striking feature of Roman legislation of the Gregorian period in regard to the tithes is its emphasis upon episcopal jurisdiction and its corresponding disregard of any rights on the part of the lower church as such. It is hard to generalize from the writings and practices of the Italian reformers, but it seems clear that they believed they were acting in accord with the canons when they assigned only the fourth of the tithe to the parish churches; the law of quadripartition left at the disposal of the bishop not only the fourth reserved for his own use but the fourths assigned to the fabric and the poor which he was authorized to administer.

The interpretation placed upon the law of quadripartition by the Gregorian reformers is most clearly illustrated by the *Liber de Vita Christiana* of Bonizo of Sutri. In Book II of this treatise, devoted to the office and duties of a bishop, Bonizo exhorts his fellow prelates not to be remiss in dispensing hospitality:

Because of this duty which rests upon the bishop, canon law has laid down this rule: that of all the revenues of the churches and of the tithes two portions shall be conceded to the bishop, one for the maintenance of his household, the other for the care of pilgrims and guests; the third part is to be assigned to the fabric of the church, the fourth to be divided among the clergy according to the merits of each.

The possibility that Bonizo is here thinking primarily of the cathedral receives support from another passage in which he cites a decree which he attributes to Pope Julius:

Of all the revenues of the church and of the tithes four parts shall be made, one to go to the bishop for the maintenance of his household, a second also to the bishop for the reception of travellers, a third to be applied to the upkeep of the church buildings, and the last to be distributed, according to merit, among those members of the clergy who dwell religiously in their houses in obedience to the bishop and without conjugal ties, being called in some churches canons, in some *ordinarii*, in others, as at Rome, cardinals.

Finally, in Book VIII, Bonizo gives a historical account of the origins of the tithe:

After the time of Constantine, with the continued growth of the Christian faith, it was decreed by the holy fathers and by the authority of the Roman Church that four portions should be made of the tithes: three of these were to be in the power of the bishop; the fourth was to be divided among the clergy according to their merits.

While Bonizo's remarks may be directed especially towards the revenues of the cathedral churches, there is implied in his exposition the claim that the bishop may divide the clerical fourth among the parochial clergy as well as among the canons of his cathedral, giving the preference to those superior in merit who live "religiously in their houses . . . and without conjugal ties," a phrase which may mean those who followed the common life.

It would probably be unwise to attach too much weight to a purely academic discussion of church revenues, written by an exiled bishop in his old age. More important is the evidence of local documents, some of which have already been cited, showing the interpretation of the rule of quadripartition that was actually followed by reforming bishops in administering the tithes of their parishes. We know that in 1058 Bishop Gerard of Florence gave a fourth of the parochial tithes to the clergy of several Florentine baptisteries who had adopted the common life. Ten years later, in judging a lawsuit in Chiusi, Pope Alexander II decided that the bishop of Chiusi must obey the precepts of canon law by giving the priest of the diocese a fourth of their tithes, retaining the other three-fourths under his own control. A third example, from a somewhat later period, should be cited with caution. In 1113 a papal legate, in trying a lawsuit between the archpriest of a Lucchese parish and a local monastery over a fourth of the parochial tithes, decided in favor of the parish church on the grounds that Bishop Anselm had formerly commanded that "all the parishes of his diocese should have a fourth of the tithes."

The practices revealed in these documents, which will be confirmed by later examples to be cited in the next chapter, are clearly contrary both to the system of tithes ordained by the Carolingian capitularies and to that sanctioned in the thirteenth century by the law of the Decretals. The discrepancy is partly to be explained as the result of the revival of ancient canon law which was then in progress, which stressed episcopal jurisdiction over church property and directed attention towards the ancient rules for the division of ecclesiastical revenues. The Roman rule, favored by the Italian reformers, prescribed, of course, a fourfold division. The assignment of a third of the tithes to the French and south Italian churches in the Gregorian period was based on the Toletan system and permitted by the papacy as a legitimate local tradition. It was also consistent with the legal outlook of the Roman reformers that they should have discarded the system of tithes ordained by the capitularies and councils of the ninth century, for the tithe had been established by the Carolingian sovereigns and the rules which gave it in its entirety to the parish churches were Frankish laws originating with the lay power and therefore suspect to the Gregorian reformers.

In establishing the principle of episcopal jurisdiction over the tithe and requiring only a fourth of the parochial tithes for the parish churches, the reformers could in practice leave most of the tithes where they actually were — in the hands of the laity and the monasteries — trusting to reforming bishops to recover them from the laity. Since the opening of the century the lay aristocracy had already surrendered many churches and tithes to ecclesiastical institutions. As early as 1019 Boniface of Tuscany and his wife Richelda restored the tithes of four parishes to the bishop of Cremona. Numerous restitutions of churches, mostly manorial chapels, were made by the House of Canossa in Mantua. Ulric-Manfred of Turin and Countess Adelaide made similar donations, the former to the extent of seriously reducing his own resources. After the middle of the century, under the impetus of the ecclesiastical reform, people of lesser rank also began to restore their share of church revenues, sometimes very small. In 1079 a priest in the diocese of Turin gave to the priory of Oulx all his rights in the parish church of Cesena, amounting to a fifth of the church and a twelfth of its tithes.

Almost invariably these restitutions were made to cathedral chapters, to monasteries, or directly to bishops, almost never to parish churches unless they had become seats of the canonical life. The founders and patrons of monasteries liked to endow them with grants of churches and tithes, enriching their protégés and at the same time gaining credit in heaven. The cathedral chapters, in which their sons were often canons, also attracted the gifts of the lay aristocracy. As a result of this preference, monastic churches and tithes multiplied rapidly during the eleventh century, eventually exciting the anger of the bishops and provoking a reaction within the monastic order itself, when the Cistercians refused to hold tithes and churches. The Gregorian reformers themselves did not object to monastic ownership of churches and tithes, provided that it did not disrupt the unity of the diocese. As Tellenbach discerned, the Gregorians were not opposed to the proprietary system as such, but solely to lay proprietorship of churches. Towards the end of the eleventh century the clerical proprietary regime, which had been created by impropriation of the lower churches, was regulated by the papacy in a form modeled upon the old laws governing the lay proprietary regime.

Thus the policy adopted by the Church in Italy in regard to parochial property was not only in accord with canon law as understood by the Gregorians, it avoided alienating the laity and benefited the monasteries who had been the loyal allies of the papacy and whose service of churches was promoting a revival of lay piety. This policy was not, of course, unique to Italy, although applied under somewhat different circumstances there. An incident which occurred at the synod of Reims in 1119 illumines the attitude of both clergy and laity which must have been general during the conflict over investitures. The second decree as proposed by Pope Calixtus II read: "We forbid to laymen investiture of all churches and ecclesiastical possessions." But much opposition arose from the laity and from some of the clergy because they believed that the Pope was endeavoring to take away the tithes and other benefices which the laity had held of old time. The opposition won the day. The decree as finally passed limited the prohibition on investiture to bishoprics and abbacies, excluding the lower churches entirely. The Concordat of Worms, which ended the struggle between Papacy and Empire in 1122, concerned solely the bishoprics and abbacies. The battle against lay proprietorship was essentially won as far as the upper churches were concerned. But the lower churches, namely the parishes and the multitudinous chapels and lesser churches, were left outside the agreements which ended the investiture controversy. The Church had won in essentials the battle against simony and clerical marriage; it had virtually destroyed the Emperor's power over the Church in Italy and had broken the opposition of the Lombard episcopate. But it had not driven the laity from their entrenched position in the rural parishes; and it had not ended the proprietary regime in the lower churches.

CHRISTIANITY AND THE STATE IN THE LIGHT OF HISTORY

T. M. PARKER

This selection from Dr. Parker's *Christianity and the State in the Light of History* not only has the value of pointing to a quantity of modern treatments of facets of the Gregorian movement, it approaches the questions involved from a longer perspective. The easy, lucid argument succeeds very well in drawing attention to the symbols or vocabulary peculiar to the eleventh century, but, because the underlying power struggle is as old as Christianity, Dr. Parker has sought to express the struggle in terms comprehensible to his own generation.

T. M. Parker was educated in history and theology at Oxford and since 1952 has been chaplain, Fellow and Praelector in Theology and Modern History, University College, Oxford. He served as Bampton Lecturer at Oxford in 1950 and as Birkbeck Lecturer, Trinity College, Cambridge, 1956–1957.

So it is not surprising to find that, by about the eleventh century, the principle of hereditary succession to feudal estates was becoming established as a custom not to be broken except as a legal punishment for crime — and custom in the Middle Ages had the force of law, indeed in Northern Europe *was* law. Nor was it land only which went by right of descent. In many cases public office followed the same rule, so that, for example, the Carolingian *comes*, the appointed representative of the king in local government, became the *comte* of the hierarchy of feudal hereditary nobility.

It seems no exaggeration to see in this development of landholding from something governed by royal will to something controlled by hereditary right, the feature which most of all marks the change from the classical unitary conception of the State to that of the State as a complex of individual or communal sharers of power characteristic of the Middle Ages proper.

It is dangerous and easy to be too precise. The idea of kingship and even the idea of sovereignty never perished wholly: the balance between centripetal and centrifugal forces varied greatly at different times and, more especially, in different parts of Western Europe. Sir Maurice Powicke, in his valuable essay entitled "Reflections on the Medieval State," has warned us, with all the authority of his unrivalled knowledge, of the danger of generalisation. We can neither generalise beyond a certain point nor dogmatise. Nevertheless no one can fail to see that in the centuries separating the Carolingian Age from that of the Renaissance men have largely ceased to think of society as a homogeneous single corporation ruled by one absolute law and a single central power. They have come rather to view it as a complex balance of different and quasi-independent centres of power, each with its own rights and duties.

At times this went to almost anarchical

lengths. The notorious formula of election supposed to have been employed by the *ricos hombres,* the highest order of nobility in Aragon, in choosing their king runs thus: "We who are as good as you choose you for our ruler and lord, provided that you observe our laws and privileges, and if not, not." The text is of doubtful authenticity but, as Hallam said, it is "sufficiently agreeable to the old government" of Aragon in practice. Aragon indeed was an extreme instance of devolution, a state in which even the right of *desnaturalización,* formal renunciation of allegiance to the Crown after due notice given, was enjoyed by all the nobility, so that political obligation was virtually reduced to a contractual basis. But, as Fritz Kern has pointed out, the same idea is in fact involved in all oaths of fealty, which were the cement of the early medieval state. "Fealty, as distinct from obedience, is reciprocal in character, and contains the implicit condition that the one party owes it to the other only so long as the other keeps faith." Always in the medieval West there is implicit the idea of rights as derived not solely from the state, but from the status of the individuals which make up the political community.

It is not difficult to see how in such an atmosphere the idea of the Church as an institution separate from the State and possessed of its own authority — an idea ultimately derived from the Biblical notion of the Kingdom of God — could develop into that of the Church as an *imperium in imperio.* So long as the classical idea of sovereignty persisted such an evolution was inconceivable or barely possible. But, given feudal conditions, the way was open. For the Church had a history infinitely longer and more impressive than that of the feudal fief. It could claim independence with far better title than any feudal landlord.

Yet this was far from being the immediate outcome of the Church's finding itself living in the new type of society which developed, as the result of a long evolution, towards the end of the first millennium A.D. On the contrary, in the breakdown of centralised power, the Church suffered a loss of independence and not without reason is the volume of the great Fliche et Martin, *Histoire de l'Église,* covering the period 888 to 1057, given the title *L'Église au pouvoir des laïques.* To understand the reasons we need to turn to a phenomenon in Church history for the elucidation of which we are indebted to comparatively recent historical scholarship — a phenomenon of which the existence was barely recognised before the nineteenth century. I refer to the notion of the "private church," the *Eigenkirche* as it is technically known. It was in October 1894 that Ulrich Stutz delivered his now classical inaugural lecture in the University of Basel entitled *Die Eigenkirche als Element des mittel-alterlich-germanischen Kirchenrechtes* (Berlin, 1895), and thereby set in motion a series of studies and controversies which have to a great extent transformed our notions of ecclesiastical development in the early Middle Ages. It is not my purpose to discuss the disputes which have arisen about the origin of the institution then described by Stutz — disputes which have been so strangely complicated and embittered by nationalistic feeling, as German and French historians have contended on behalf of Teutonic and Latin claims to the doubtful honour of inventing the private church. (These contests remind one of the rivalry between Ipswich and Sudbury to be regarded as the original of Dickens's Eatanswill, for only an idealist could regard the private church as a blessing to mankind or to the Church.) It would probably now be agreed that Stutz's attempt to identify the institution he discovered with a peculiarity of Germanic paganism carried on into early German Arian Christianity and thence into medieval Catholic polity has failed, and that the proprietary church is but one example of the phenomena produced by the general decay of centralism in the decline and fall of the Roman Empire in the West. Let us content ourselves with considering its importance in the history of Church-State relations.

What was an *Eigenkirche?* It was a church built by a landlord on his estate for the spiritual benefit of himself and his dependents. In accordance with the spirit of the times the Dark Ages landlord regarded his foundation as his own property and both Church and State perforce admitted his claim to possess it. Not only was the church and its income his, but he retained also the right to nominate its priest — a right which has survived in this country and in some other parts of Europe in the form of lay parochial patronage, even though other vestiges of the private church system have vanished. In its heyday the landlord claimed not only to appoint but to control his priest. Furthermore, he conceived himself to possess the right to dispose of his church by gift, sale or testamentary disposition, to third parties, if he did not leave it to devolve upon his heir. Short of secularising the building (which would have been sacrilege) he could do almost anything with it, whilst over its incumbent his powers were often greater than those of the diocesan bishop.

The obvious friction between lay and ecclesiastical authority occasioned by this claim of the laity to the ownership of what were to become the parish churches of medieval Europe needs no stressing. What is of even greater significance is the extension, by a natural transition of thought, of a parallel claim to lay control of the larger units of ecclesiastical jurisdiction and property, bishoprics and monasteries. Kings and lesser magnates, accustomed to the idea of owning and controlling churches upon their domains, thought it natural to claim similar rights over the sees and religious houses they had in many cases founded or endowed and of which in any case they were the protectors. In regard to bishoprics there was the earlier precedent of imperial and royal con- trol of episcopal elections to aid their claim: monarchs had long been accustomed to think of the bishops of their realms as *their* bishops. With the decline of royal power in favour of that of local lords, it was equally natural for these latter to regard the greater churches within their sphere of influence as subject to them. So one finds a curious rivalry between kings and nobles for the control of episcopal elections. For example, of 77 sees in eleventh-century France, the king had the control of about 25: the rest were in the hands of dukes, counts or viscounts. That control was exercised chiefly in determining the occupant of the see. The temporal lord might either concede the election to the clergy and people, subject to his own confirmation, or himself appoint a candidate direct. But it did not limit itself to this. The idea of the private church, as we have seen, involved more than the mere right of appointment to it: the church was the lord's property. This notion, too, is applied to bishoprics. The see, with its lands and property, comes to be regarded as an "honour"; the same word is used as that increasingly current to describe a lay fief. As such it is in the overlord's gift. He expects from its tenant homage, fealty and military service: he claims the right to invest him with the honour and when it is vacant take it "into his own hand" until the time comes to grant it again to its newly chosen incumbent.

Here we come face to face with another aspect of the influence of feudal ideas upon ecclesiastical affairs. When political power is localised to the extent required by a feudal organisation of society, and is bound up with the holding of land, it is inevitable that the Church should become, to a greater degree than ever before, a sharer in that power. For, before the development of money investments and finance, endowment of the Church can only be in land. And when land is the measure of power, the greater ecclesiastical landlords, bishops, abbots, cathedral

churches and other prelates or corpora-
tions, must of necessity be important units
in the State, responsible for military service, local jurisdiction, and supervision of
agricultural economy. And if they are
such, the State cannot be indifferent to
their identity. Even in their spiritual capacity, as men wielding great powers of
spiritual persuasion and coercion, bishops
and other prelates are formidable and we
have already seen that the State, from the
moment it became Christian, interested itself profoundly in ecclesiastical appointments. But when to spiritual power was
added, under feudal conditions, temporal
authority over wide areas of territory, bishops and abbots became personages about
whose loyalty the State could not take
chances. In England the prince-bishop in
the full sense, as found in, for example,
Germany, was a rare, indeed a unique
phenomenon. Yet who can look at Durham Castle and reflect upon the key position of the Palatinate of Durham in the
defence of the Scottish border without
realising that no King of England could
remain indifferent to the outcome of an
election to that see?

The temporal importance of prelates was
the ultimate and legitimate reason upon
the State's side for its retention of at least
some degree of control over ecclesiastical
personages and property, a control which
came to be regarded by zealous churchmen as out of harmony with any adequate
notion of the Church's freedom. For the
Church, too, had a strong case for demand-
ing self-government. The State, in making ecclesiastical appointments, was not
likely to pay great heed to spiritual qualities, as compared with docility to state
policy, skill in administration or even
warlike ability. (It is one of the ironies
of history that Bruno of Toul, who was
to become the first of the great eleventh-
century reforming Popes as Leo IX, owed
his elevation to episcopal rank chiefly to
his powers of generalship.) Nor was this
the worst possibility. An unscrupulous
ruler might sell ecclesiastical office as
readily as temporal to the highest bidder,
so countenancing and encouraging the peculiarly deadly sin of simony. Equally
the general neglect in the later Dark Ages
of the canons prohibiting clerical marriage,
combined with the general drift towards
hereditary office, opened the possibility of
feudal warrior-priest dynasties of Has-
monean type. A feudalised Church meant
a Church dominated by lay power and
lay mentality, and also set up serious ob-
stacles to a spiritual revival such as the
low clerical morals of the age, so horri-
fically depicted in the lurid pages of St.
Peter Damian's Liber Gomorrhianus, quite
obviously demanded.

These inner contradictions of a feudalised Church did not at first become apparent when in the tenth and eleventh
centuries, as the disorders brought about
by the second great wave of barbarian invasion died away, men of the better sort
set their hands to Church reform. There
were so many obvious Augean stables to
cleanse that the ultimate question of the
source of the troubles of the Church did
not need to be faced. Attention has often
been drawn recently to the great contrast
between these first reform movements and
what we are accustomed to call the Hildebrandine spirit. The distinction lies
chiefly in the fact that before the middle
of the eleventh century the reformers concentrated upon extirpating the more glaring abuses, with a certain indifference to
the means by which this could be effected.
If emperors and kings were willing to use
their power directly to put down simony
and to recall the clergy to a higher standard of life, well and good. Even though
such a method of reform meant some per-
petuation, or even extension, of lay control of the Church, they did not object to
it, provided that it was effective, and they
were the more easily able to maintain this
attitude in that they retained an idea of
kingship as divinely ordained for the
Church's benefit.

But when Hildebrand became Pope in
1073, under the title of Gregory VII, a

change was almost at once perceptible, a change to be attributed almost solely to the powerful personality of one of the most original figures of the Middle Ages. Of the two greatest reforming zealots of the period immediately preceding, St. Peter Damian (who died in 1072) and Cardinal Humbert (who had disappeared from the scene some ten years earlier), only the latter can be considered in any real sense a precursor of the great Pope in his views. Damian held to the old tradition. He wished for collaboration between Pope and Emperor in the work of reform, a union so close that "the King shall be found in the Roman Pontiff, the Roman Pontiff in the King," for, as he said, "in one Mediator of God and man, these two, the *regnum* and the *sacerdotium,* are bound together by a divine mystery." A similar ideal had been held in the previous century by Pope Silvester II (the famous Gerbert of Aurillac) in his close alliance with the Emperor Otto III. Damian held on to a hope which in the eyes of Hildebrand came to be forlorn and, indeed, based upon illusion. Damian could even exhort the young Emperor, Henry IV, destined to become Hildebrand's bitter enemy, to show himself a new Constantine, a title he had earlier, and with better reason, accorded to Henry's father, Henry III. Yet even Damian had believed the Roman Church to be superior, not only to every other ecclesiastical authority, but to every lay power also, and enunciated the maxim, *Terrenus imperator non habet in Romana Ecclesia potestatem.* [The earthly ruler has no jurisdiction in the Roman Church.] This thought was developed much more powerfully by Cardinal Humbert, who used the comparison, which became a commonplace later in the Middle Ages, of soul and body as expressing the true relations of the spiritual and temporal powers. It was for the spiritual power, as the directing force of the body of Christendom, to decide what should be done, for the temporal to put the decisions into effect.

Here we see already adumbrated the germ of the Gregorian ideas. Nevertheless, Gregory VII carried the seminal notions of his predecessors in reform much further than they. It would seem that he felt driven to do so by a realisation that the temporal heads of Christendom were bruised reeds. In a letter written within four months of his accession one indeed finds him comparing the spiritual and temporal powers to the twin eyes of Christendom and his earliest negotiations with Henry IV (already under papal ban before Hildebrand became Pope) are marked by a desire for good relations. In the view of Fliche, it was not until two years later, in 1075, that Gregory, almost in despair, turned to a more intransigent policy, which was marked by the decree of February 1075, forbidding lay investiture of bishops with their sees, and by the document known as the *Dictatus Papae.*

Let us consider the scope of these two pronouncements. Lay investiture, the juridical act symbolised by the giving of the episcopal ring and staff to the elected bishop, was the means by which the "honour" of a bishopric was conferred, and this demonstrated in the most vivid way possible the control claimed by the temporal power over local church, accompanied as it was by the spoken formula, *Accipe ecclesiam tuam.* It had already been forbidden, though in rather vague terms, by Nicholas II in 1059. Gregory had hitherto not enforced this decree and had recognised bishops appointed by lay investiture. Though we do not possess the exact terms of his prohibition of 1075, it seems clear that it must have been more precise and formal than that of his predecessor, and therefore to be regarded as a declaration of war against a custom regarded hitherto as a normal expression of royal authority in the Church.

Far more significant, however, is the teaching contained in the *Dictatus Papae,* a list of papal prerogatives drawn up in succinct and aphoristic form. An Italian scholar, G. B. Borino, has recently made the interesting suggestion that this series of short sentences was originally the list of *capitula* attached to a catena of canonical *auctoritates* collected at Gregory's orders to give precedents for the programme he proposed to follow. The supposition is very probable when one considers the degree to which the whole reforming movement saw itself as an attempt to restore the Church's forgotten canon law. The articles of the *Dictatus* are largely concerned with papal supremacy over the Church and may indeed have been determined largely by the attempts Gregory had been making to persuade the Eastern Church to recognise papal authority. But the document also lays down in its twelfth article that the Pope has the right to depose emperors. It is noteworthy that Caspar, who has traced canonical precedents for most of the other propositions in it, found none for this. It would be interesting to know, if Borino's idea is correct, what texts were originally cited under this heading in the canonical collection to which, as he conjectures, the *Dictatus* supplied headings.

Here, indeed, is something novel. Arquillière, describing it as *une conclusion théologique nouvelle,* remarks with reason: "This is real theocracy, and all the attempts which have been made to deprive Gregorian thought of this characteristic will always come up against this short and formidable formula."

With the enunciation of a theory of spiritual supremacy over temporal affairs began the great contests between *regnum* and *sacerdotium* which are the central interest of medieval history between the eleventh and the fourteenth centuries. To describe them in detail would be wearisome and unprofitable, and would add nothing to a task many times performed by others. One fact must be noted. The quarrels began with what is loosely termed the Investiture Contest, extending from the days of Gregory VII to the settlement achieved between his successor, Calixtus II, and the Emperor Henry V, Henry IV's

son, in 1122, the Concordat of Worms. The expression is unhappy because, as the late Professor Z. N. Brooke argued, the original dispute between Hildebrand and Henry IV turned far more upon freedom of episcopal elections than upon investiture itself. It was Gregory's successors who turned it into a contest about investiture and the right of monarchs to grant to ecclesiastics the temporal possessions annexed to great churches. In so doing, Brooke argued, they lost sight of what Gregory had been chiefly anxious to secure, namely, the Church's right to select its own higher personnel. The principle behind lay investiture was far greater than that of the ceremony itself and it was lost sight of in the struggle. Moreover, as suggested earlier, it was a matter upon which both Church and State could put forward a plausible case: indeed in the matter of appointments to sees and abbeys the internal contradiction implicit in the fact of a feudalised Church was at its most acute, for the men whose choice was in question had by force of circumstance to be great figures in Church and State alike. Only once, it would seem, was the question roundly faced, in 1110 and 1111, when, on the occasion of Henry V's coronation, the unworldly Paschal II proposed a solution of the problem by which the Church would renounce temporal possessions in return for the abandonment by the State of all claims upon the selection and control of prelates. The proposal outraged alike ecclesiastics reluctant to abandon worldly position and lay magnates wishing to retain full rights of patronage and control of local churches, and the idea collapsed in scenes of riot. Nevertheless the root of the difficulty was then uncovered, even if all men shrank from recognising it.

With the settlement, or patching up, of the investiture dispute by an agreement which left to the Emperor the substance of his claim to nominate prelates at the price of his more shadowy right to invest them with the symbols of power, the essential dispute changed character. More and more the point at issue is the theoretical relationship of the spiritual and temporal powers. This was the heart of the matter in the struggle between Frederick Barbarossa and the Holy See, and in the later epic conflict between Frederick II and the Papacy, even though many concrete political issues, such as the status of the Italian city states, entered in. At the time the question was commonly posed in directly theological terms. Does the Emperor hold his power directly from God, or only mediately through the Pope? Nowadays it would probably be differently phrased. Are Church and State aspects of one society or are they two independent powers? In either case, are there two sources of authority on earth or one only? In some such way as this the problem — which has been with us ever since — would present itself to a modern mind.

It is, however, important to notice, in order to understand a vital difference between medieval assumptions and our own, that the former question was never asked in that precise form in the Middle Ages. It is always common ground to both sides in Church-State disputes that there is one Christian society only, one Christendom, one *respublica Christiana*. (For example, Gregory VII, in his simile of the two eyes of Christendom, mentioned above, speaks of the *sacerdotium* and the *imperium* as two *dignitates* in the one body of the Church. On the other hand, one of his opponents, the author of the treatise, *De unitate ecclesiae conservanda,* wrote a treatise accusing him of causing schism in the Church by excommunicating the Emperor.) The idea of unity is the starting point of all discussion of the subject: what is in dispute is the relationship between the two principles distinguished within that unity, the spiritual and temporal powers, *sacerdotium* and *regnum*. From at least the time of Pope Gelasius I in the fifth century the existence of these two principles, corresponding to the dual nature of man, body and soul, spirit and

matter, had been recognised: indeed Gelasius's affirmation of the independence of the two powers, each in their own sphere, became a *locus classicus* in later discussion. But, as all experience of condominium shows, it is easier to assert the existence of parallel authorities than to determine their relations and the limits of their power. In this specific case it was all the more difficult to do this, in that the distinction could easily become too absolute. To say, as was commonly done, that it was the State's function to direct man to his earthly goal, the Church's to prepare him for heaven, was to overlook the fact that on Christian principles no act of man, however mundane, is without relevance to his eternal destiny, and that no supernatural human activity, be it never so spiritual, is without repercussions upon his everyday life. (This last consideration is perhaps best illustrated by the fact, familiar to every medieval man, that even withdrawal from the world in order to pursue a life of heavenly contemplation is an act which may have far-reaching effects upon society. Monasticism was one of the most important social phenomena which had to be taken into account by every medieval state.)

If we have been right in supposing that, when first an alliance of Church and State upon Christian terms became possible, the problem posed by the Christian conception of the Church as a supernatural society existing nevertheless partly in visible form on earth was never roundly faced, then we shall understand more easily why the great contests of Church and State in the eleventh and following centuries were, in a sense, predestined to occur. For the first attempt to solve the half-recognised problem was, as we have seen, to continue half-consciously the relationship between civil society and religion of pagan days, making the necessary adaptations by makeshift means. In the gradual transformation of Western Europe, begun by the barbarian invasions and deepened by later insecurity, the difficulties evaded earlier became acute. Hence the sharp conflict we have been considering.

It is easy to say that by greater good-will on either side the crisis could have been averted. But that is really an histor-ical subterfuge. No doubt there is some truth — not to say truism — in the asser-tion. But the fact that the same phrase forms today the cheapest and most unillu-minating homiletic comment upon con-temporary troubles, varying from labour unrest to the schism between Eastern and Western ideologies, suggests that it is al-ways superficial. Men are most usually quarrelsome when they are in perplexity, and no mere exhortations to charity, which do nothing to lighten the obscurity which is straining it, effect anything of value. In the case we are considering this banal com-ment about the need for good-will ignores the series of unresolved contradictions in medieval Church-State relations. To one of these attention has already been drawn. It lies in the fact that whilst an unen-dowed Church would have had very little chance of independence in an insecure age, that very endowment, necessarily in terri-tory, involved the Church ineluctably in mundane concerns and so drew upon it the jealousy of the civil power. But two others remain to be noticed.

There is first the consideration that it was not only the position of the Church as feudal landowner on a large scale which hampered the efforts of the eleventh-cen-tury reformers to free the clergy from worldly cares and lay control. There was also the fact that in the West, in contrast to Byzantium, there was no educated laity capable of staffing a civil service, which had therefore to be clerical in composition. We speak loosely of conflicts of Church and State at this time, meaning conflicts of clergy and laity, forgetting all too easily that those who upheld the rights of the State were themselves predominantly clerics. The most anti-clerical medieval king or emperor would have been helpless in any conflict with the Pope without his own clerks to argue his case. This, no less than the civic importance of prelates as

landholders, made the claim of the medi-eval clergy to the status of an international privileged caste, exempt from lay jurisdic-tion and control, an anomaly.

Finally, at a deeper level, there lay the fact that the clergy claimed — and was bound to claim if it was to fulfil its apos-tolic commission — a power of censorship over lay morals. Now politics, as everyone up to Renaissance times would have agreed, is a part of morals. If so, ecclesi-astical censure must necessarily sometimes involve indirect interference in the sphere normally appropriated to the temporal power. And such interference would be the more arbitrary in that centuries of dealing with a semi-barbarous society had imbued the Church with the spirit of the stern parent or schoolmaster, rather than that of the urbane spiritual adviser, in dealing with its children. It proceeded by means of excommunication and penitential discipline rather than by exhortation when breaches of the moral law were in evidence, and expected the State to enforce its cen-sures by the weight of the secular arm if need be. How can the independence of the State from the spiritual power be a reality when the State is thought of as standing to the Church in the relation of child or pupil?

This last was the issue which really lay behind the contest over the relations of *regnum* and *sacerdotium*. In the last re-sort, the power of the Pope over kings or emperors, by whatever metaphysical or technical theological arguments it may be defended, rests upon the papal pastoral mission. "These different arguments," says M. Arquillière of Gregory VII's polemic, "tend towards a single end, which is seen by him with a clear inevitability": to show the pre-eminence of the priesthood over the royal office as that of the "father" over the "son" or of the "master" over the "dis-ciple." "The royal office is in the Church. It exists for the Church; even dynastic heredity does not give it a right which may not be touched. . . . In the last resort it exists by the Church. . . . This [Gregory's attitude] is the exercise of the power of the keys, in a society where the accepted faith recognises no other limit to it than the sanctity of its usage." As the same author rightly says, "we come here upon the bases of medieval civilisation." So he can claim, if perhaps with some exaggeration, that "if we wish to keep profoundly within the atmosphere of the age, as the historian must always try to do, we cannot say that Gregory VII thought that he was committing the least usurpation. He never goes outside his strictly spiritual attitude. Only, kingship, in assuming, chiefly with Charlemagne, a weighty religious mission — in absorbing into itself the old idea of the Empire, in making of itself a magistrature spiritual as much as political — kingship thus conceived was condemning its representatives one day or another to be dominated by the supreme head of the Church."

The wheel has come full circle. The king who sought, or felt it his duty, to control the Church, by that very fact finds himself subject to the Church's judgement. The fateful sequel to lay control of ecclesiastical matters noted by Arquillière was necessarily involved by the social evolution of a religion which by its charter deeds committed, not to kings, but to apostles, the spiritual guidance of its adherents. The medieval crisis of Church and State is in the last resort but the acute perception of the dilemma almost necessarily involved, that the State must either dominate the Church or be dominated by it.

CHURCH, KINGSHIP,
AND LAY INVESTITURE IN ENGLAND
1089–1135

NORMAN F. CANTOR

The short, self-contained statement from Norman F. Cantor's *Church, Kingship, and Lay Investiture in England, 1089–1135* is a recent interpretation of this great movement. Dr. Cantor takes an extreme position and without beating about the bush places the "investiture struggle" first among the four great revolutions between the eleventh and twentieth centuries. He considers the movement to have passed through the now accepted classical cycle — radical and destructive at first, the slowing down of the initial impetus, and, lastly, the seizure of the revolution by largely self-interested politicians. Professor Cantor, born in Canada and educated at the University of Manitoba, Princeton and Oxford, is a member of the history faculty of Columbia University. He has promised in the preface of the present work, two more volumes to develop fully the history of the mediaeval English Church after the Conquest.

My own interpretation of the investiture controversy is very much indebted to the work of Tellenbach, but it gives even more universal significance to the intellectual conflicts of the period.

It has been characteristic of the history of the West that its destiny has been shaped by four world-revolutions in which previous tendencies culminated and from which new ideas and systems emerged. By a world-revolution I mean a widespread and thoroughgoing revolution in world-view, the emergence of a new ideology which rejects the results of several centuries of development, organized into the prevailing system, and calls for a new right order in the world. In modern history these world-revolutions are well known — the Protestant Revolution of the sixteenth century, the liberal revolution of the eighteenth century, the Communist revolution of the twentieth. The investiture contro-versy constitutes the first of the great world-revolutions of western history, and its course follows the same pattern as the well-known revolutions of modern times.

Each of the world-revolutions has begun with some just complaint about moral wrongs in the prevailing political, social, or religious system. In the case of the investiture controversy the leaders of the revolution, who have been called the Gregorian reformers, complained about the domination of the church by laymen and the involvement of the church in feudal obligations. This system had led to severe abuses, especially that of simony, which came to be defined in its most general sense as the interference of laymen with the right ordering of church offices and sacraments. In their condemnation of simony as heresy, the Gregorians had a perfectly valid complaint.

It has been characteristic of all the world-revolutions, however, that while each has begun by complaining about abuses in the prevailing world order, the ultimate aim of the revolutionary ideologists has been not the reform of the prevailing system, but rather its abolition and replacement by a new order. In the case of the investiture controversy, complete freedom of the church from control by the state, the negation of the sacramental character of kingship, and the domination of the papacy over secular rulers, constituted the ideal new order.

As in the case of all other world-revolutions, the ideology of the Gregorians called forth violent opposition on the part of both vested interests and sincere theoretical defenders of the old order. After many acrimonious disputes and a flood of propaganda literature, bitter and protracted warfare resulted. The polarization of educated society into revolutionary and conservative left a large group of uncommitted moderates, including some of the best minds of the age, who could see right and wrong on both sides.

As in the case of all other world-revolutions, the ideologists of the investiture controversy were only partially successful in creating the new order. They succeeded in destroying the old system, but the new world was not the revolutionary utopia. Rather it was a reconstruction of the political and religious system which took into account both old and new elements and left room for the human limitations of greed and power. The church gained a large measure of freedom from secular control, and there was a noticeable improvement in the moral and intellectual level of the clergy. But the church itself, from the time of the investiture controversy, became more and more interested in secular affairs, and the papacy of the high Middle Ages competed successfully for wealth and power with kings and emperors. The church itself became a great super-state governed by the papal administration.

As in the case of all other world-revolutions, the ideologists during the investiture controversy were themselves united only upon the most immediate and more limited aims of the revolution. As the revolution proceeded, the Gregorians divided into a moderate and a radical wing, each led by eminent cardinals. The radicals were headed by Humbert and Hildebrand, the moderates by Peter Damiani. As in the modern world-revolutions, the radicals were for a short period in control of the Gregorian reform movement, a period which was long enough to destroy the old order. But as the conservatives and moderates of various complexions perceived at last the real aim of the radicals and their reckless disregard for consequences, the radicals lost their leadership and were unable to realize their utopian ideals.

As in the modern world-revolutions, the radicals lost their leadership not to the moderates of their own group, whom they had earlier swept aside, but rather to the politicians, the practical statesmen, who called a halt to revolution and tried to reconstruct from the shattered pieces of the old system and the achievements of the revolution a new and workable synthesis which would again make progress possible. This tendency is already evident during the pontificate of Urban II in the last decade of the eleventh century, and it became dominant in the papacy during the 1120's.

Like all world-revolutions, the investiture controversy never reached a final and complete solution. New ideas in a new generation made former issues less meaningful and the men of the new generation turned to other interests and new problems. Just as Voltaire and Hume could not understand why the men of the sixteenth and seventeenth centuries should have fought over abstruse theological principles, so already in the 1130's a canon of York Cathedral could not understand why Anselm and Henry I should have quarrelled over lay investiture two decades before.

The age of the investiture controversy may rightly be regarded as the turning-point in medieval civilization. It was the fulfillment of the early Middle Ages because in it the acceptance of the Christian religion by the Germanic peoples reached its final and decisive stage. On the other hand, the greater part of the religious and political system of the high Middle Ages emerged out of the events and ideas of the investiture controversy.

CLUNY AND THE INVESTITURE STRUGGLE

THEODOR SCHIEFFER

Dr. Schieffer has had a notable professional career. After taking his doctorate, he spent several years on the staff of the *Monumenta Germaniae Historica*. (See Note page IX of *Introduction*.) After military service during World War II he became professor of Mediaeval history at the University of Cologne. Besides the portion taken from a public lecture delivered at Paris and published in the *Revue historique*, Professor Schieffer has published several monographic studies on European problems from the eighth to the tenth centuries.

THE role that the great Abbey of Cluny was destined to play before and during the Investiture Struggle, it seems to us, was certainly very complex. It is impossible to resolve the problem by means of any ready-made formulas. The Cluniacs and the Gregorian reformers ought neither to be confused nor ought they to be separated. That which, in the attitude adopted by the abbot of Cluny, may seem contradictory, uncertain, and inconsequential, can be explained however, without great difficulty, if we do not lose sight of the fact that the expression "Investiture Struggle" embraces several different phenomena: ecclesiastical centralisation, achievement of jurisdictional primacy in spite of the opposition of metropolitans and bishops, all of these are not of the same magnitude as the clash between the *Imperium* and the *Sacerdotium* and the revolutionary attempt to create a new order under the banner of pontifical theocracy! One has to take into account this difference, this polarity, to comprehend correctly what must have been the line of Cluny. By creating a very intense atmosphere of piety, by depending on pontifical authority and by escaping from the system of episcopal authority, the Cluniacs unconsciously contributed to preparing the Investiture Struggle. But nothing could be more incorrect than to attempt thereby to interpret the investiture conflict as a victory for the Cluniacs. On the contrary, Cluny was a victim — perhaps — *the* victim of this struggle. Cluny was a significant manifestation of this late period of the Middle Ages, which had its roots in the pre-Gregorian period, in an order established upon harmony, even upon the unity of the temporal and spiritual. By the Investiture Struggle, which came to fracture or at least to make uncertain this unity, the Cluniacs saw themselves swept into a crisis out of which they could find no way. Truly it is not a matter of chance that this crisis put an end to the brilliant era of Cluny and that the great abbey had to surrender to others its role of protagonist of monasticism.

Reprinted from "Cluny and the Investiture Struggle" by Theodor Schieffer (*Revue historique*, 1961). [Translated by the editor of this volume.]

THE CONFLICT BETWEEN
CHURCH AND STATE

KARL F. MORRISON

Karl F. Morrison, a portion of whose "Introduction" to *Imperial Lives and Letters of the XI Century* appears below, is the most recent commentator on the Gregorian epoch. Trained at the Universities of Mississippi and Cornell, Dr. Morrison's interpretation makes use of a wealth of materials emphasized by the school of the history of ideas. Dr. Morrison is currently on the faculty of the University of Minnesota.

THIS concept of the pontifical king, so highly cherished by the Salians, was theoretical in origin and in written exposition, but its practical ramifications were of the utmost significance. If the king were actually "head of the Church," he could be certain of benefiting directly from the vast material resources of the Church. These were, in fact, central to the protection of the royal prerogative. So Conrad II, with the cooperation of Bishop Warrmann of Constance, had Ernst [I] of Swabia excommunicated by the spiritual authority of the Church and then hunted down by its material power. So, too, Henry IV found ecclesiastical resources indispensable in the Investiture Controversy, as his own letters witness. It was in the ceremony of investiture that the king, bestowing the symbols of ecclesiastical power, and receiving vows of fidelity from those upon whom the symbols were bestowed, received also his greatest claim to ecclesiastical support.

A contemporary of Henry IV defended lay investiture on the grounds that the king acted during the ceremony in a purely secular capacity, as "head of the people," and that as such he deserved, for the sake of the common interest, to know the man to whom he had entrusted the defense of his city; after all, this same thing had been done long before by "kings who were not anointed and by mayors of the palace." This position, however, would probably have been distasteful to the Salians themselves and to their more "reactionary" supporters. Henry IV, for example, was fully aware of the pontifical significance of his title when he wrote as "King by the grace of God to Udalrich the monk" and demanded that the former abbot of Lorsch give to his envoy his staff of office (Letter 3); the authority which had made the abbot unmade him. Wenrich of Trier went yet further and claimed "pontificacies and priesthoods" for his ruler; the Scriptures, he wrote, showed that among the Maccabees, Alexander had established Jonathan high priest, and Demetrius, Simon. In what way, therefore, were the claims of Henry excessive? And even more telling is the account given by Radulf Glaber of the show of confidence Henry III rendered to an abbot, anonymous in the chronicle. Henry said to the abbot, " 'Set aside the staff of pastoral rule, which you believe ought to be used at a mortal man's giving.'

Reprinted by permission from the "Introduction" by Karl F. Morrison to *Imperial Lives and Letters of the Eleventh Century*, edited by Robert L. Benson (Columbia University Press, 1962).

When the abbot had cast it from him, the King took it up, and placed it at the right hand of an image of the Savior. 'Go,' he said to the abbot, 'and receive it from the hand of the Omnipotent King, and nevermore be the debtor of any mortal for it, but use it freely, as befits the exalted height of so great a name.' " If the account be true, and it seems to represent Henry's opinions well, it is clear that Henry believed generally that when he invested ecclesiastics with the ring and the staff he acted as a representative, a vicar, of the "Omnipotent King" and as the head of the worldly affairs of the Church. And the recipients of those symbols were his "debtors." His handling of the staff indicates that he believed that, just as power was delegated to him by the King of Kings, so he, and he alone, might return it to its source, and thus, with the good pleasure of God, the power was fully his as long as he chose to retain it. The concept of the pontifical king, the king as the temporal head of the spiritual order as well as of the secular State, therefore, received its practical expression in the ceremony of lay investiture, just as it received its theoretical expression in the rite of coronation.

Although the scope of its aims and dissatisfactions was vast, on this precise point of practical expression the reformed Papacy, insisting on the purely lay character of kings, the spirituality of investiture, and the sinfulness of mixing the two, chose to join battle. The weapons it used were drawn from that province peculiar to itself upon which temporal powers might not encroach, the province of spiritual authority. Its arsenal of tradition was fully as strong as that of the kingship. St. Paul, with curious impartiality, furnished essential Scriptural support for the spiritual as well as for the temporal power, for he wrote: "But he that is spiritual judgeth all things, yet he himself is judged of no man" (I Corinthians 2:15). Patristic weight was also given to this position. Hosius of Cordova, for example, had vehemently admonished Constantius II that the Empire

and the Church were two distinct institutions, though both were of common divine ordination, and that each had its own sphere of interest. In sacred things, the emperor was to be instructed by the Church, and not to be its master. St. Ambrose, gainsaying Optatus of Milevis, maintained that the emperor was within the Church as its son, not over it as its lord. And St. John Chrysostom affirmed that the spiritual power stands as high above the secular as the heaven does above the earth, or even higher.

Kings were special objects for the exercise of the spiritual censure; for it was generally maintained with St. Isidore of Seville that "the name of king is held . . . by virtue of upright action; it is lost through sinning." The spiritual arm, according to those jealous of its power, as judge of right-doing and of sinning, was also capable of judging when a king had forfeited his office through his sins. These wicked kings, who inflicted "the greed of spendthrift government and very cruel dominion" upon their peoples, were "tyrants." Such rulers, consumed by vice, were inflicted by God upon peoples for their shortcomings, according to St. Augustine, and were to be endured as divine chastisement.

Subsequently, however, the attitude of the Church inclined toward the subversion of tyrants, rather than toward submission to them. Of kings, Pope Nicholas I wrote to Aventius, bishop of Metz, "See whether they govern according to right; if they do otherwise, they are to be considered tyrants, rather than to be regarded as kings. We are bound to resist these men, and to rise up against them, rather than to be subject to them." Shortly before the time of Nicholas, Louis the Pious had been deposed for his sins and for leading his people "to their common destruction, although he ought to have been a leader of salvation and peace for this very people." His judges were bishops, "vicars of Christ and key-bearers of the kingdom of Heaven."

This was the tradition adopted by Gregory VII, who divided kings into two classes: those who "are the body of Christ, the true King," that is, those who serve the Church; and those who are "the body of the Devil," or those who seek their own good and engage in oppression of the Church. It was in the vigorous maintenance of this position, which made the Church the judge of which kings were worthy and which were not, that Gregory "ruffled and bestirred himself very notably."

The Salians had certainly been forewarned that their concept of kingship would not be acceptable to all persons in all places. When Henry III, for example, had affirmed that through his priestlike unction, he had received power to govern "before all others," Wazo, bishop of Liége, answered him in the tones of an adversary. "This unction of yours," he said, "is other than you affirm it to be, and far different from the priestly; for through it you have been arrayed for slaying, but we, through the action of God, for vivifying; wherefore, by as much as life is more excellent than death, by that much, without doubt, our unction is superior to yours." And while Henry IV envisaged himself as David, Gregory VII held before him the alternate figure of Saul, who was "cast aside by the Lord."

St. Stephen of Hungary had written: "It is not fitting for any save men of faith, and imbued with the Catholic Faith, to accede to the order of regal dignity." And Henry IV confessed that deviation from the Faith was the sole reason for which he could be deposed. Gregory, too, adopted the position that orthodoxy (which meant for him obedience to the Roman Church) was the major criterion for receiving and for losing royal power; and from this position he launched his attack upon Henry. When, despite continued warnings, Henry insisted on preserving his rights of investiture in Milan and elsewhere, Gregory took the unprecedented steps, first, of declaring lay investiture heretical and sacrilegious, and thereafter, of excommunicating a king

of the Romans, an emperor-designate, because he persisted in the practice.

Because he would not sacrifice that position as the head of the episcopal order which tradition had handed down to his forebears, and which, cherished by them, was transmitted finally to him, Henry became for Gregory, a "member of Antichrist," a fosterer of heresies; he had deviated from the true Faith. He had betrayed the trust of that position as defender of the Church which he had accepted with the kingship; he was an enemy of God and the Holy Church, a tyrant to be resisted, not obeyed. He was cut off from the living body of the Church.

The political effects of this action were immense even though it was completely within the spiritual sphere, for the excommunication of Henry, as Mirbt has shown, was in itself the equivalent of formal deposition; and further, the "civil" deposition of 1080, Schmeidler has demonstrated, was actually nothing other than ecclesiastical proceedings against a king who because of his official functions had been excommunicated as unjust and tyrannical, and so unworthy to rule. The denial of the Eucharist and of "Christian communion" to Henry, the charges of injustice brought by the Papal legate against him, the extortion of the holy relics (the imperial insignia) from him, and his own eagerness to be reconciled with Rome strongly support this view.

In the decrees against lay investiture, Gregory had claimed for the priesthood that shadowy region where the temporal mingled with the spiritual, so long claimed and held by the pontifical kingship; and from this action there ensued the turmoil and the bitter conflicts in which Henry IV and his son passed their reigns, the conflicts in which the strength of the kingship was ruinously spent.

Still, in these conflicts, the Pope was only striving for supremacy in the Church, and the King, for supremacy in the State. Their aims were reasonable; indeed, except in the most unusual circumstances, it had always been agreed in Western Europe, that the pope was the spiritual head of the Church, a spiritual institution, and that the king was the temporal head of the State, a temporal institution. New factors were introduced in the eleventh century, however, and from them arose the Controversy. The first of these new elements was the equal strength of the two political entities, the Papacy and the German kingship. In earlier times, the moral and, to a greater degree, the material weakness of the Papacy had invited intervention in Papal affairs by the German king, the "emperor [or emperor-designate] of the Romans." By advancing their program of ecclesiastical reforms, by allying with the Normans on their southern borders, and by consolidating their control of Papal estates, however, the reformer popes had brought the Roman Church to a high level of moral and material strength; the conditions which once gave the secular arm opportunity for intervention in its affairs had been removed. At the same time, the German kingship was restored through the assiduity of Henry IV to a remarkable vigor, after its decline during his minority. This restoration was facilitated by two major elements, the introduction of certain feudal relationships between lord and liegeman, and the existence of the Ottonian State-Church system; the second is generally considered to have been of greater importance than the first. This ecclesiastical system in which prelates were regal (or Imperial) vicars, in which their officials were officials of the State, in which their material resources were at the service of the temporal ruler, in which the king was "the head of the Church," was a central element of the restored regal power. On the one hand, there was the Papacy with its new concepts and power; on the other, the German kingship, with its power revived largely through the instrumentality of tradition. Their positions were largely (though not irreconcilably) antagonistic, and for the first time each had the material resources with which to defend its proper position.

The second new element was the redefinition of the "Church" by the reformers in such a way as to conflict sharply with the Ottonian State-Church system, and their attempt to implement their new definition. According to the theories fully expressed by Pope Gelasius I (492–496), and grown axiomatic by the eleventh century, man consisted of two parts, the soul and the body. The soul, as the vivifying element, was superior to the body; so the institution whose province was the spiritual was superior to that whose province was the physical. The Roman Church, by divine ordination, was at the head of the spiritual institution. To this concept, Gregory VII and his followers added the refinement that the province of the spiritual power extended to whatever affected the spirit; therefore, by logical extension, it included the material world and the governing of states. By this extension, Gregory claimed supremacy over all secular rulers, and indeed, the supremacy of any exorcist or priest over an emperor. By this redefinition, all ecclesiastics were in all matters subject primarily to their spiritual Lord, the Christ, and to His earthly vicar, the Roman pontiff. No longer were prelacies and abbacies to be at the disposal of the temporal lord and their resources at his services.

To Henry, this new attitude presented very considerable peril. If the imperial churches were taken from him, it was certain that the supreme authority in his kingdom would fall to the princes, as, in fact, it threatened to do at any rate. But while the Church of his realm with its immense resources remained as his support, there was good hope for the effectual maintenance of the ancient character of the king as the head of the State. Clearly, then, Henry opposed the Gregorian reformers for his own political and economic survival. He readily acknowledged the spiritual supremacy of the priesthood over nonpriests; he did not oppose ecclesiastical reforms, but to the contrary, he showed some zeal for them. On the point of the subjection of the Church to the temporal ruler in material affairs alone he could not afford to yield.

In Italy, where some of the richest parts of Henry's realm lay, the Papacy, with its new material strength and its refurbished theoretical weapons, and the German kingship, with its newly regained power and its traditional concepts, first met in conflict. Battle was joined on the long-festering issue of the Milanese archepiscopacy. In 1071, when Henry seemed to have gained victory over his chief enemies in Germany, the Saxons, Guido, the archbishop of Milan, died, and the aristocratic party, nobles and clergy, elected a certain Godfrey as his successor. Godfrey was invested by Henry and consecrated in 1072; but the "popular" party, the Patarini, had also elected an archbishop, Atto, who was consecrated by Pope Alexander II, without investiture by imperial agents. Because Henry refused to abandon Godfrey, five of his intimate advisers were excommunicated in 1073, charged with responsibility for their master's action and attitude. In the same year, a grave revolt by the Saxons forced Henry to make conciliatory gestures toward the new Pope, Gregory VII, so as to be able to devote his attention and resources fully to his problems in Germany; consequently, he renounced Godfrey and acknowledged Atto. Henry's victory over the Saxons on the Unstrut in 1075, the reascendancy of the aristocratic party in Milan, and the death of Atto made possible Henry's reassertion of his prerogative in Milan in 1075. The aristocratic party elected Tedald the new archbishop, and, in direct defiance of the decree against lay investiture which Gregory had issued from his Lenten Synod earlier in the year, Henry conferred investiture upon him through a deputized legation. He went even further and instructed this same legation to appoint and to invest bishops for Fermo

and Spoleto, both of which lay within Papal territory, and then to seek to win Norman support away from the Papacy. The new principles of the reformed Papacy and its new material strength were thus simultaneously challenged by the conventional prerogative of the German king; the challenge was vigorously accepted, and the two powers came into bitter conflict.

Yet there were many central points upon which Henry and his foes agreed: the divine institution of the kingship, the obligation of rulers to undertake the defense of the Church, the interdependence of kingship and priesthood, the secular occupation of rulers, and the spiritual occupation of priests. The violence which Henry suffered and that which he perpetrated followed, however, from a struggle for headship in the Church, from a basic difference in concepts of the proper world order.

Pontifical kingship, in which the ruler had control of those aspects of the Church which appertained to this world, agreed ill with the position of the reformers that restrictions imposed upon any aspect of the activity of the Church limited also the freedom with which the Church might serve its spiritual function and, in fact, distorted that very function. In their view, the influence of the ruler in the internal affairs of the Church was untoward and must be removed; his claims to such influence, based on his position as "a sharer of the priesthood," must be destroyed. He must be seen as a layman, crowned as king as much through the ministry of priests as by the will of God; his unction must be clearly nonpriestly; his position, nonecclesiastical. His mind must no longer be both kingly and priestly. And stripped of all traces of pontificalism, he must be unequivocally a son, a spiritual subject of the Church — its defender, its liegeman. In this way, the supremacy of the spiritual authority would be vindicated.

Nothing could have been more unacceptable to the royalists. The Scriptures and the tradition of the Fathers pronounced the king, elect of God, crowned of God, vicar of God, the anointed of the Lord, bearer of the episcopal ring as well as of the material sword, one whose power was ordained of God, whom the very Scripture called a "minister of God." They prescribed obedience to him as a religious duty. How, therefore, could the king rightly be stripped of his ecclesiastical character? By the very command of God, one might not lift one's hand against the Lord's anointed. The kingship was unalterably an ecclesiastical, a pontifical office, as well as, or rather because it was, the supreme temporal office; and the king, in whose person the character of temporal power was joined with that of ecclesiastical authority, was rightly the "head of the Church."

In the last analysis, though they held much in common, the two positions were irreconcilable; there could be but one head, the regal pontiff or the pontifical king.

SUGGESTIONS FOR ADDITIONAL READING

To assemble a reasonably modern bibliography for this period, the reader is referred to the following works to be found in any college library: A. Fliche, *La Réforme grégorienne et la Reconquête chrétienne 1057-1123* (Paris, 1940), pp. 7-11 (Vol. 8 in A. Fliche et V. Martin, *Histoire de l'Eglise depuis les Origines jusqu'á nos jours*); A. Fliche, *La Querelle des Investitures* (Paris, 1946), pp. 217-221 in the series, *Les Grandes Crises de l'Histoire*, edited by J. Calmette [this is Professor Fliche's last publication on this subject]; *Cambridge Medieval History*, bibliographies at the end of Vol. 5, *Contest of Empire and Papacy* (the literature to 1924); Austin Lane Poole, *From Domesday Book to Magna Carta*, 2nd ed. (Oxford, 1955); J. P. Whitney, *Hidebrandine Essays* (Cambridge, 1932), pp. 59-68; Paul Vinogradoff, *Roman Law in Mediaeval Europe*, 2nd ed. (Oxford, 1927); Walter Ullmann, *The Growth of Papal Government in the Middle Ages* (London, 1955); *English Historical Documents*, Vol. II, pp. 589-597, edited by David C. Douglas and G. W. Greenaway.

There are many excellent books in English on this period but no great work of synthesis like that of Fliche's three volumes *La Réforme grégorienne*. The narrative history of the period can be read in two old works not lightly to be disregarded, Neander's *General History of the Christian Religion and Church*, Vol. 7, translated by Joseph Torrey (Bohn's Standard Library, London, 1852), and Henry H. Milman, *History of Latin Christianity*, Vol. 4, 3rd edition (London, 1872). The most convenient and authoritative presentation is to be found in the *Cambridge Medieval History*, Vol. 5, which may be read in a condensed version in C. W. Previté-Orton, *The Shorter Cambridge Medieval History*, Vol. 1 (Cambridge 1952).

For information on the popes of the period, though regrettably uncritical, are Vols. 6-8 of Horace K. Mann, *The Lives of the Popes in the Middle Ages*, 2nd edition (London 1925). On Gregory VII, J. P. Whitney, *Hildebrandine Essays* (Cambridge, 1932) is judicious and especially helpful for bibliography while all of Fliche's books need to be consulted on individual popes.

Walter Ullmann, *The Growth of Papal Government in the Middle Ages* (London, 1955) has provided a most valuable work weaving together several strands of the weightiest continental publication in the history of ideas, political theory, and history of canon law. The bibliography is rich for sources and for discussion but it cannot be recommended for the beginner. For a simple sketch of canon law, R. C. Mortimer, *Western Canon Law* (Berkeley, Calif., 1953) together with Z. N. Brooke, *The English Church and the Papacy* (Cambridge, 1931), provide a guide through the maze of collections so difficult for the modern student to grasp. For an example of how the canon law of the Gregorian period was put together, the monograph of J. J. Ryan, *Saint Peter Damiani and His Canonical Sources* (Toronto, 1956) [Pontifical Institute of Medieval Studies, *Studies and Texts* 2] is excellent.

With the works on the papal histories and the canon law, R. W. and A. J. Carlyle, *History of Mediaeval Political Theory in the West*, Vol. 4, and Paul Vinogradoff, *Roman Law in Mediaeval Europe*, 2nd edition (Oxford, 1929) may be read most profitably.

For recent German scholarship on our subject besides G. Barraclough, *The Origins of Modern Germany*, 2nd edition (Oxford, 1948), see Barraclough, *Mediaeval Germany*, 2 vols. (Blackwell's,

Oxford, 1938) and the other volumes of that series, F. Kern, *Kingship and Law in the Middle Ages* (1939) and G. Tellenbach, *Church, State and Christian Society at the Time of the Investiture Contest* (1940).

An extremely perceptive study with excellent illustrative materials on simony can be found in R. W. Southern, *The Making of the Middle Ages* (New Haven, 1955), now reprinted in a Yale paperback. For the detailed working out of taxation of ecclesiastical property see Catherine F. Boyd, *Tithes and Parishes in Medieval Italy* (Cornell, 1952).

Two helpful works for the history of Cluny are: Joan Evans, *Monastic Life at Cluny 910–1157* (Oxford, 1931) and Rose Graham, *English Ecclesiastical Studies* (London, 1928). On the relations between property control and ecclesiastical reform is the enlightening article of G. Mollat, "La Restitution des Églises Privées au Patrimoine Ecclésiastique en France du IXe au XIe Siècle," in *Revue Historique de Droit Français et Etranger*, 4me Ser. 27e Année, pp. 399–423 (1949). For information and interpretation of the lives of the German Emperors see Robert L. Benson, ed., *Imperial Lives and Letters of the Eleventh Century* (Columbia Univ. Press, New York, 1962). A portion of Dr. K. F. Morrison's "Introduction" is used in the selections but the entire work is well worth reading for the latest "Idea-historical" interpretation of Germanic kingship. Dr. Morrison has re-evaluated the position of Gregory VII in an article, "Canossa: a Revision," in *Traditio* Vol. XVIII, pp. 121–148 (1962).